The Civilization of ancient China

THE CIVILIZATION OF ANCIENT CHINA

THE ILLUSTRATED HISTORY OF THE ANCIENT WORLD

THE CIVILIZATION OF ANCIENT CHINA

JOHN CHINNERY

ROSEN

This edition published in 2013 by:

The Rosen Publishing Group, Inc.
29 East 21st Street
New York, NY 10010

Library of Congress Cataloging-in-Publication Data

Chinnery, John D.
The civilization of ancient China/John Chinnery.—First [edition].
pages cm.—(The illustrated history of the ancient world)
Includes bibliographical references and index.
ISBN 978-1-4488-8502-2 (library binding)
1. China—Civilization. I. Title.
DS721.C535 2013
931—dc23
2012034519

Manufactured in the United States of America

CPSIA Compliance Information: Batch #W13YA: For further information, contact Rosen Publishing, New York, New York, at 1-800-237-9932.

Editor: Peter Bently
Designer: Rebecca Johns
Picture Editor: Julia Ruxton
Managing Editor: Christopher Westhorp
Managing Designer: Manisha Patel
Commissioned Artwork: Cecilia Carey and Jantje Doughty (motifs), Sallie Alane Reason (map), Yukki Yaura (calligraphy)

Captions for pages 1–4

Page 1: Covered blue and white bowl with *bogu* floral decoration; early 18th century, reign of Kangxi.

Page 2: A glazed terracotta, five-clawed imperial dragon from a frieze in the Forbidden City, Beijing.

Page 3: Gold filigree headdress fitting, late Ming dynasty, ca. 1600.

Page 4: Avalokiteshvara as Guide of Souls, ink on silk. From Cave 17 at Mogao, near Dunhuang, China, early 10th century CE.

龍

CONTENTS

INTRODUCTION

China: The Great Survivor

OPPOSITE
The fertile Yellow River valley in Qinghai province. The name "China" derives from the first imperial dynasty, the Qin, but the Chinese call their country Zhongguo ("Central Country"). When China was divided into smaller states, before unification under the Qin in 221 BCE, this term referred to the states in the central part of the Yellow River basin.

China is the only ancient civilization to have survived up to the present day. It was able to flourish on an extensive area of flat river basins, notably the Yellow River basin in the north and the Yangzi River basin in central China. Both these rivers flow from west to east across the breadth of the country. Other substantial rivers, such as the Pearl, flow from mountain ranges in south and central China down to the South China Sea.

This unique geographical setting provided all the material and human requirements necessary for the development of civilization. Since Neolithic times the great majority of Chinese have occupied the flatlands of the great river basins and the mountain valleys. They have subsisted in the main on cereals (millet and later wheat and maize in the Yellow River basin and contiguous regions, and rice in the Yangzi valley and farther south) and vegetables, supplemented by poultry, pork, and fish. Dairy products, which play such a major role in the West and in South Asia, were not part of their diet, and even now mutton and beef are rarely eaten in some parts of the country. Ancient China had more forests than exist today, but in more recent times a shortage of firewood on the plains led to the Chinese habit of chopping food into small pieces, so that it can be cooked quickly and economically. This was an important factor in the development of China's unique cuisine.

BELOW
The landscape of China has inspired artists for centuries. This scene by Hu Youkun (17th century) is in the "boneless" style, using wash but no outline. Normally used for flowers, the technique lends the work an ethereal quality.

China is bounded to its west and southwest by sparsely inhabited grassland and desert as well as massive mountain ranges. These areas were not impassable, and over the centuries traders and Buddhist missionaries and pilgrims often traversed them both westward and eastward along recognized routes. The most famous route was the Silk Road, so named because traders used it to transport much sought-after silk fabrics to western Asia and Europe. However, the distances were so great and relatively devoid of

logistical infrastructure that there was never any danger of China being invaded from the west. Nomadic tribes from the north, such as the Mongols and Manchus, were occasionally able to assemble powerful and highly mobile armies to conquer China. But as the leader of one such invasion indicated, they could conquer China on horseback but they could not rule on horseback: it was only possible to govern the country by adopting Chinese cultural and political systems.

BELOW
During the Shang and Zhou periods the casting of bronze artifacts for ritual purposes became highly skilled (see pages 26–29). This bronze ritual axe bears the stylized, staring face of a type known as *taotie*, a mysterious motif found as early as the Erlitou culture of the late Neolithic (see page 16).

A UNIQUE CIVILIZATION

Beginning with Neolithic prehistory and concluding with the last imperial dynasty, the Qing, this is a survey of Chinese civilization from the earliest times to the beginning of the twentieth century. It is illustrated throughout with outstanding examples of China's rich heritage of art in a great range of media, including architecture. The arts of China are unique and highly distinctive in character, and in times past they were so widely admired by its neighbors that for centuries China was viewed as the "mother culture" of East Asia, whose culture exerted a strong influence on surrounding peoples from Korea and Japan to Vietnam. But this did not mean that China's artists and artisans were closed to foreign influences, either in terms of technique, media, or subject-matter. For example, Iranian techniques of silversmithing were adopted eagerly under the Tang (see page 102), and *cloisonné* also came via western Asia from its ultimate origin, Byzantium (see page 168). From the seventeenth century, Chinese painters were influenced by Western styles of painting introduced by Jesuit missionaries at the Qing court. Throughout most periods of Chinese history there was an openness to innovation, at least in certain regions or among certain groups of artists, that served only to enrich China's material culture.

Another characteristic of Chinese civilization is its high level of technical skill, which developed early in prehistory and continued through the centuries. In terms of quality of workmanship, the bronze vessels the Chinese produced some three thousand years ago have never been surpassed to this day, and it was many centuries before the West

A map of present-day China. The People's Republic occupies essentially the same area as the last imperial dynasty, the Qing. Most provinces of modern China have long existed as distinct cultural regions, but they became formal administrative units only under the Ming, whose 13 provinces and two metropolitan regions (centered on the Ming capitals of Nanjing and Beijing) largely persist today (though two Ming provinces were split to make 17 in all). The incorporation of Tibet, Mongolia, Manchuria, Taiwan, and Central Asian lands under the Qing added another 11. Today 30 regional divisions have provincial status: three metropolitan regions (Beijing, Shanghai, Tianjin), 22 provinces, and five autonomous regions (Xizang, Xinjiang, Ningxia Hui, Neimongol, and Guangxi).

KEY

XINJIANG	Province/autonomous region
A.R.	Autonomous Region
N.H.A.R.	Ningxia Hui Autonomous Region
●	City
■	Metropolitan city
▲	Sacred mountain
✲	Other site of cultural importance

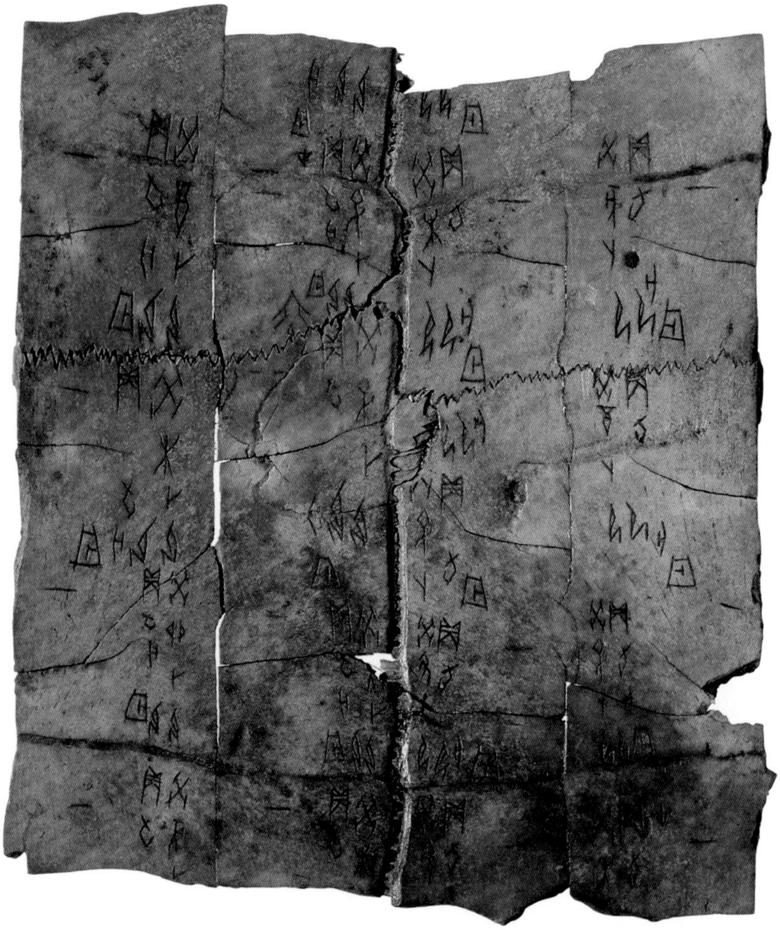

ABOVE
The earliest surviving examples of writing appear on the Bronze Age "oracle bones" of the Shang dynasty (see page 21). On these bones the pictogram origin of many characters—literally pictures of what they represent—is often clear. Oracle bone, Shang dynasty, ca.1500–ca.1050 BCE.

learned the secret of producing true translucent porcelain to match the quality of Chinese porcelain of the eleventh century. The Chinese were the first to cast iron and forge steel, the first to make paper and gunpowder, the first to use the compass, and the first to print books. In many respects they were technically ahead of western Europe until the Industrial Revolution of the eighteenth and nineteenth centuries.

THE CHINESE LANGUAGE

Another unique aspect of Chinese civilization is its writing system. There are wide divergences in the spoken language, which consists of dialects sufficiently distinct from each another as to be considered separate languages (Cantonese, Shanghainese, or Wu, and Mandarin, for example). In addition there are countless subdialects. However, for literate Chinese these linguistic differences have always been of less importance because Chinese is written not phonetically but ideographically, so the same script can be read in any dialect. All Chinese dialects consist broadly of the same stock of meaningful syllables, each of which is represented by a character. Although the syllables may very widely in pronunciation (for example, the numbers one to three are *yi*, *er*, *san* in Mandarin and *yat*, *yi*, *sam* in Cantonese), they are always written with the same character. So while it takes considerable effort to become literate in Chinese, the writing system has the advantage of being used by all Chinese, no matter which dialect they speak. This has helped the Chinese to maintain their national identity over the centuries.

The Chinese writing system is over three thousand years old, making it the world's oldest writing system still in use. Since its emergence in the Bronze Age its basic characteristics have not changed, even though the forms of individual characters have evolved. China's first imperial dynasty, the Qin (221–206 BCE), standardized the script, and subsequent dynasties maintained the tradition of a unified system, so that even today it is still possible to understand Chinese writings dating back two millennia. The sheer number of Chinese characters and the great variety of their forms provided a fertile ground for the development of the art of calligraphy, which to this day remains a major art in China, one at which even emperors strove to excel (see pages 110–113).

In this volume Chinese words are written in Hanyu Pinyin ("Chinese Spelling"), or pinyin for short. This romanization system was introduced by China's government in the 1960s to establish an international norm and to standardize the pronunciation of Putonghua ("Common Speech"), the variety of Mandarin that has been promoted as a national standard language for general use in government, education, and the media. Pinyin is simpler than earlier romanization systems but a few letters need explanation. For example, c is pronounced *ts*, q is roughly *ch* (as in *chin*) and x is roughly *sh* or the *ch* in German *ich*.

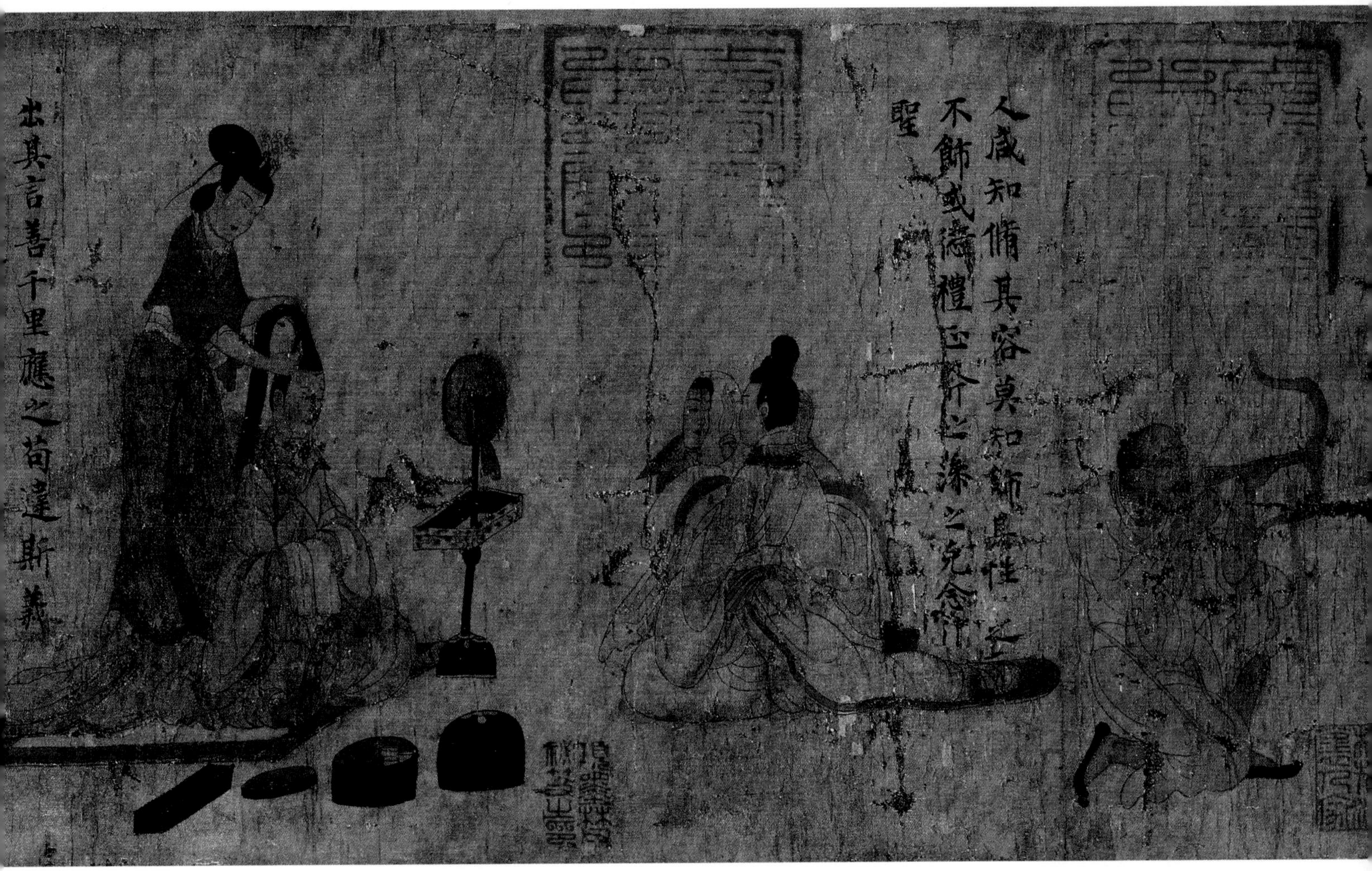

BELOW
The Admonitions of the Instructress to the Court Ladies (detail), a copy of a long scroll by the Jin-dynasty painter Gu Kaizhi (344–405). Gu was famed for portraits that succeeded in conveying both the likeness and character of the subject. None of his original work survives. (See also page 64.)

一

CHAPTER ONE

BEGINNINGS

FROM THE
EARLIEST TIMES
TO 221 BCE

夏

CRUCIBLE OF A CIVILIZATION

Prehistory and legend to ca. 1500 BCE

OPPOSITE
An earthenware jar with striking painted designs discovered at the late Neolithic site of Machangyuan in Minhe county, Qinghai province. Majiayao culture, ca. 2200–2000 BCE.

夏 The earliest precursor of humankind in China dates back about 1.7 million years and was an example of *Homo erectus* known as Yuanmou Man. Somewhat later, about 250,000 to 400,000 years ago, came the famous Peking Man (*Homo erectus pekinensis*), whose remains and other artifacts were found in a cave at Zhoukoudian (Choukoutien) near Beijing (Peking) in the 1920s. Peking Man could apparently use fire, and the large number of animal bones and fruit seeds found in his cave showed that he was a typical hunter–gatherer. Unfortunately, the important human remains discovered at Zhoukoudian were lost during the Second World War.

At the same site, at a higher level, were found some of the earliest remains of modern humans (*Homo sapiens*). By then people could make fire as well as use it, and they also possessed many more advanced hunting weapons, such as bows and arrows, and harpoons for catching large fish. They fashioned domestic utensils of stone, bone, and horn. There is evidence that the early modern humans of Zhoukoudian already had a concept of the soul and its continued existence after death.

From about 10,000 years ago, at the begining of the Neolithic period (New Stone Age), the inhabitants of what is now China advanced to living in relatively large village communities, practiced slash-and-burn farming, plowed the land, and kept domesticated animals such as dogs, pigs, and chickens. Their technology also became more complex and included weaving, carpentry, pottery using the potters' wheel, and copper smelting. In the late Neolithic (from about five thousand years ago) the population spread rapidly and different clans occupied different regions. This led to clan rivalry and conflict and the rise of clan leaders, who built fortified castles for their own defense.

BELOW
Fish are among the designs on this painted bowl discovered at Banpo near Xi'an in Shaanxi province. The bowl was used as part of a coffin cover. Yangshao culture, Neolithic period.

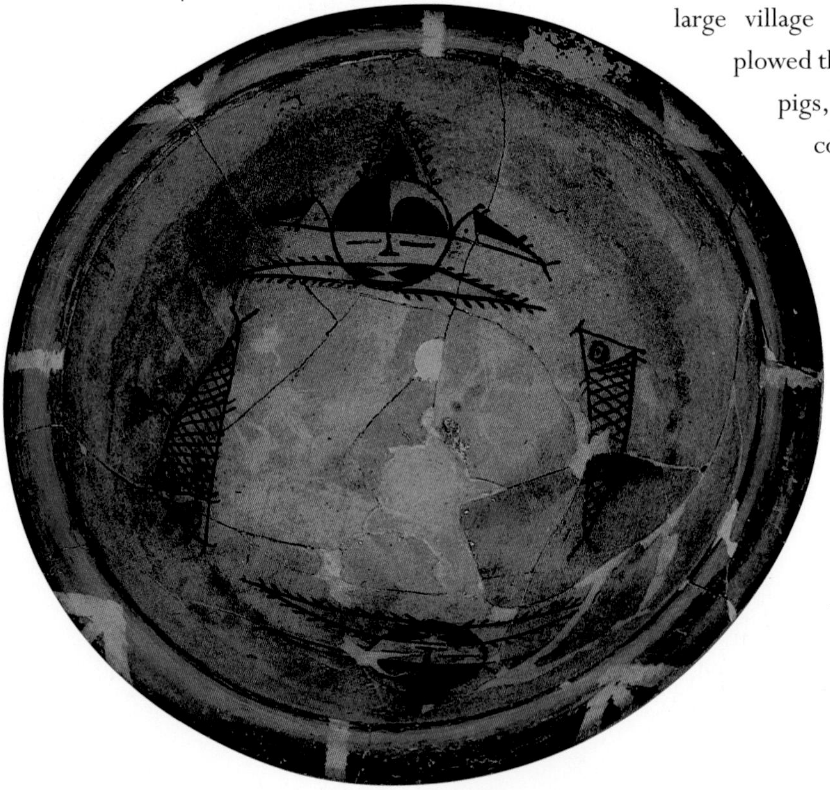

ARTS OF NEOLITHIC CHINA

The most distinctive artifacts by which China's various Neolithic regional groups can be identified

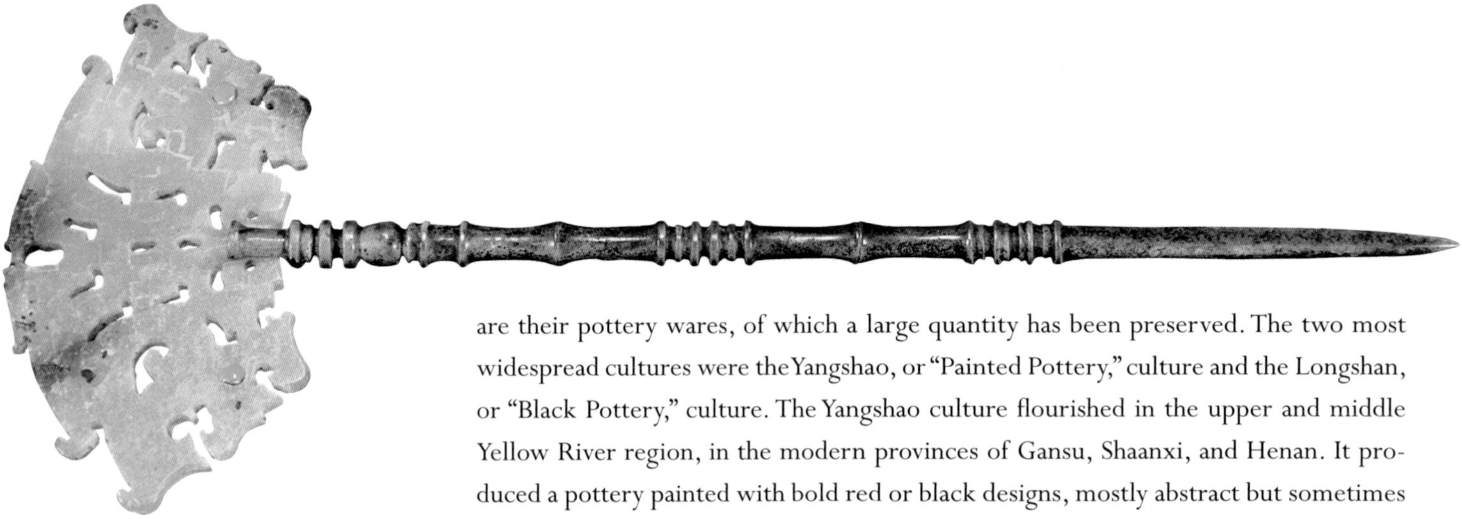

ABOVE
A hair ornament found in 1989 in a tomb in Shandong province. It lay next to the skull of the tomb's occupant, but it is uncertain whether it was worn in life or made specifically as a funeral object. The burial site was one of the largest of the late Neolithic Longshan culture. Jade with turquoise inlay, ca. 2000 BCE.

are their pottery wares, of which a large quantity has been preserved. The two most widespread cultures were the Yangshao, or "Painted Pottery," culture and the Longshan, or "Black Pottery," culture. The Yangshao culture flourished in the upper and middle Yellow River region, in the modern provinces of Gansu, Shaanxi, and Henan. It produced a pottery painted with bold red or black designs, mostly abstract but sometimes with human faces, animals, birds, or fish (see illustration, page 14). The fish designs are the forerunners of some of the decoration on modern Chinese pottery.

The later Longshan culture was first centered in the modern province of Shandong in the east of China. As its name suggests, the culture produced black pottery; this was hard and of very high quality, being thinly walled and fired at a higher temperature than the Yangshao ware. The Longshan people eventually spread westward, and examples of their black wares have been found in the middle Yellow River region, overlaying the native Yangshao artifacts.

At the end of the third millennium BCE a third Neolithic culture, the Erlitou, was centered in Yanshi county, Henan province, where a number of bronze vessels were found at the site from which the culture is named. These are the earliest bronzes to be discovered in China. The Erlitou also produced artifacts of jade, or nephrite, a hard, translucent stone, which was white, gray-green, or green in color. Much prized by the Chinese through the ages for its beauty and durability, it was considered to embody the qualities of purity, humanity, justice, and courage. It was worked throughout the Neolithic period. Some jade objects were purely decorative, but others had a ritualistic purpose. It is probable that the ancestor cult, China's longest lasting and most widespread religious practice, dates back as far as this period.

MYTH AND LEGEND: THE XIA DYNASTY

According to Chinese myth, the first rulers of China were the famous "Three Sovereigns," named Fuxi, Shennong, and Huangdi, culture heroes who brought the arts of civilization. Their successors were said to have been the "Five Emperors," who presided over a golden age of good government. The fifth of these rulers, Emperor Shun, was concerned to bring an end to a long period of continuous floods, and appointed a figure known as Yu the Great to find a means of controlling the waters of China's great rivers.

After toiling for thirteen years, Yu eventually succeeded by digging artificial waterways to drain the water into the sea, wearing himself out in the process. He was noted for his selfless dedication to his task and in the course of his labors he is said to have passed his home several times without being tempted to take a rest.

To reward Yu, Shun appointed him his successor, the first emperor of the Xia—China's first dynasty, according to tradition. Yu is said to have reigned for seven years before being succeeded by his son. Whichever elements of this legend are true—and people still visit the supposed tomb of Yu near Shaoxing in Zhejiang province—it is fairly well established that a tribe called the Xia achieved dominance over China's central plains in the twenty-first century BCE. This coincided with the period of the Erlitou culture and it is possible that Erlitou was indeed the center of Xia power.

The legend of Yu the Great also emphasizes an abiding concern of Chinese rulers down to the present time: how to tackle the floods that periodically devastated the plains, often as a result of heavy snow in the headwaters of the rivers. The need to organize communal action to tackle flooding was always a major concern of Chinese governments, and is seen today in the controversial Three Gorges project, which aims to prevent flooding of the lower Yangzi.

RIGHT
Discovered in 1959, the site of Erlitou in Henan province produced the earliest known Chinese bronze artifacts, including this bronze ornamental plaque with turquoise inlay in the form of an animal mask. It is about six inches (14.4 cm) long. Erlitou culture, ca. 2000–1600 BCE.

商

SERVANTS OF THE SUPREME LORD

The Shang Dynasty (ca. 1500–ca. 1050 BCE)

BELOW
This finely carved late Neolithic "monster" face combines human-like features with large tusks or fangs. Such faces were the subject of great curiosity in later periods, although their original purpose is unknown. They may have been amuletic, designed to ward off evil and bring good fortune. The face resembled the *taotie* faces that appeared on the vessels of the Shang and Zhou dynasties, and perhaps served a similar purpose. Jade, late Neolithic, ca. 2000 BCE.

The Shang tribe originated in present-day Shandong in eastern China and subsequently moved their capital twice, first to Zhengzhou in east Henan province and later farther west up the Yellow River. In Zhengzhou the remains of the Shang city wall are as much as 60 ft. (18 m) thick. The walls appear to have been aligned north to south and east to west, a characteristic of Chinese cities throughout history. The excavators of the site also found molds for producing bronzes, as well as many bronze and pottery artifacts. Some bronze had been produced toward the end of the Neolithic period, for example by the Erlitou culture (see pages 16–17), but the Bronze Age in China is reckoned to begin with the Shang, which conquered the last Neolithic settlements ca. 1500 BCE.

After their second move the Shang conquered the Xia and founded the Shang dynasty (ca. 1500–ca. 1050 BCE). They established their capital near modern Anyang and for more than 500 years spread their influence over a great area of north and central China. This was China's first historical dynasty—the first to be fully authenticated by written texts and archaeological evidence. The Shang built upon the achievements of the late Neolithic culture of Longshan (see page 16), as is demonstrated by the similarities between the two cultures, such as walls constructed of tamped earth and divination using "oracle bones" (see page 21), although the bones used by the Longshan bore no inscriptions.

Shang society was hierarchical and aristocratic, with the king at its head. Shang aristocrats were given titles and sometimes territories to control, but were always subject to the Shang king. The king and aristocracy drove two-horse chariots to war and the hunt. Their weapons included powerful retroflex bows, which were also used for hunting deer, wild oxen, bears, tigers, and wild boar, which at that period were quite plentiful. Such luxuries were not available for the common people, who still lived and worked much as their Neolithic ancestors had done.

RIGHT

A bronze *lei* vessel, a type of wine jar, with stylized patterning and animal designs. The Shang used many types of bronze container to offer food and drink to their ancestors, but the details of ceremonies associated with the containers are not known. Three-dimensional animal forms were a feature of southern vessels. Late Neolithic–early Shang period, ca. 18th–11th century BCE.

RIGHT
This ivory *bei* (beaker), elaborately decorated with turquoise inlay, was discovered in the tomb of Lady Hao (Fu Hao), the wife of the late Shang dynasty king Wu Ding (ruled ca. 1215–1190 BCE). Women wielded considerable power in the Shang state—Lady Hao is described on inscriptions in her tomb as having been a military commander.

Shang religious practices were concentrated on the veneration of their ancestors, who were induced, through sacrifices and prayers, to help the living. Some sacrifices were carried out at fixed dates, others as the occasion arose. The most important ones were on the anniversaries of dead kings. The grandest rites were conducted by the king, and sometimes involved the sacrifice of as many as forty oxen for one royal ancestor. Sacrificial offerings involved the use of often elaborate bronze vessels (see pages 26–29).

BELOW
The ancient Chinese prized bronze and jade more highly than gold, which was mainly applied as ornament. But from the Eastern Zhou it was used more widely for independent objects, such as this astonishing cast openwork sword hilt. Too fragile to be practical, it was probably a display or funerary item. Eastern Zhou, ca. 500 BCE.

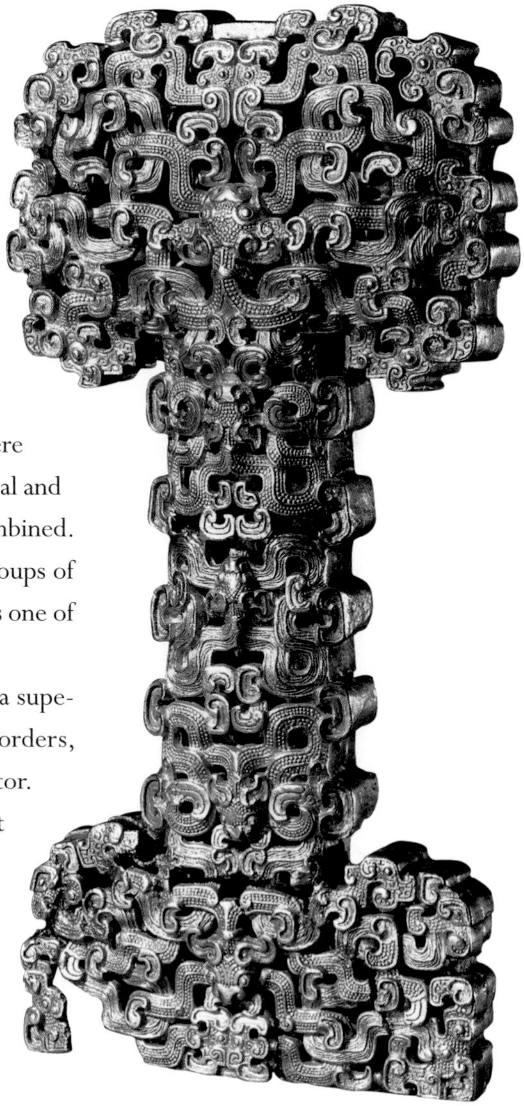

THE ART OF DIVINATION

The king sought to communicate with his ancestors by the use of oracles. More than 100,000 "oracle bones," mostly the shoulderblades of oxen or the lower shells of tortoises, have been recovered. When the king consulted the oracle, his question for the ancestor was inscribed on the bone, which would then have a hole drilled into it. A hot metal bar was pressed into the hole, causing the bone to crack, and an augur would interpret the cracks to determine the ancestor's reply. The reply was then inscribed on the bone. The bone inscriptions are the earliest surviving examples of the Chinese script and amount to China's first historical archive. Some questions concern state affairs, such as auspicious times for hunts or military expeditions, but the king also asked personal questions about births, dreams, illnesses, and even toothache.

Shang rulers entrusted divination to a sort of college of soothsayers, who were also in charge of the calendar. The Shang employed two number systems—decimal and duodecimal—that are still in use today in various contexts, either separately or combined. The decimal system was the basis of the calendar, used for counting days and groups of ten days, repeated through the year. The official name of each Shang king includes one of these ten numbers, denoting the day on which his sacrifice had to be conducted.

As well as the ancestors, divinations also served other cults. One involved a superior deity called Shangdi (Supreme Lord), protector of the natural and human orders, including cities and armies, who seems to have been regarded as a remote ancestor. There were other deities: gods of the four compass points, mothers of the East and West, sacred mountains, the Yellow River, and so on. Shamans and sorcerers abounded and there were also numerous local popular animistic cults.

The Shang kings were buried together with so-called "companions in death"—close companions, horses and chariots, and fully armed guards. In addition, humans of the lower social orders might be put to death as sacrificial offerings. These practices died out in the succeeding Zhou dynasty.

AN AGE OF PHILOSOPHY AND WAR

The Zhou Dynasty, ca. 1050–221 BCE

BELOW
This bull's head was found in what may have been a horse and chariot burial next to tombs near Luoyang, the Eastern Zhou capital. The tombs were likely those of Zhou kings, hence the high quality of the bronzes discovered there. The ox head was probably an ornament from a chariot shaft. The eyes were originally set with glass, now disintegrated. Bronze with gold and silver inlay, Eastern Zhou period, 4th–3rd century BCE.

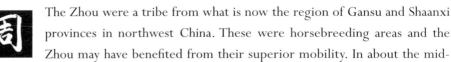

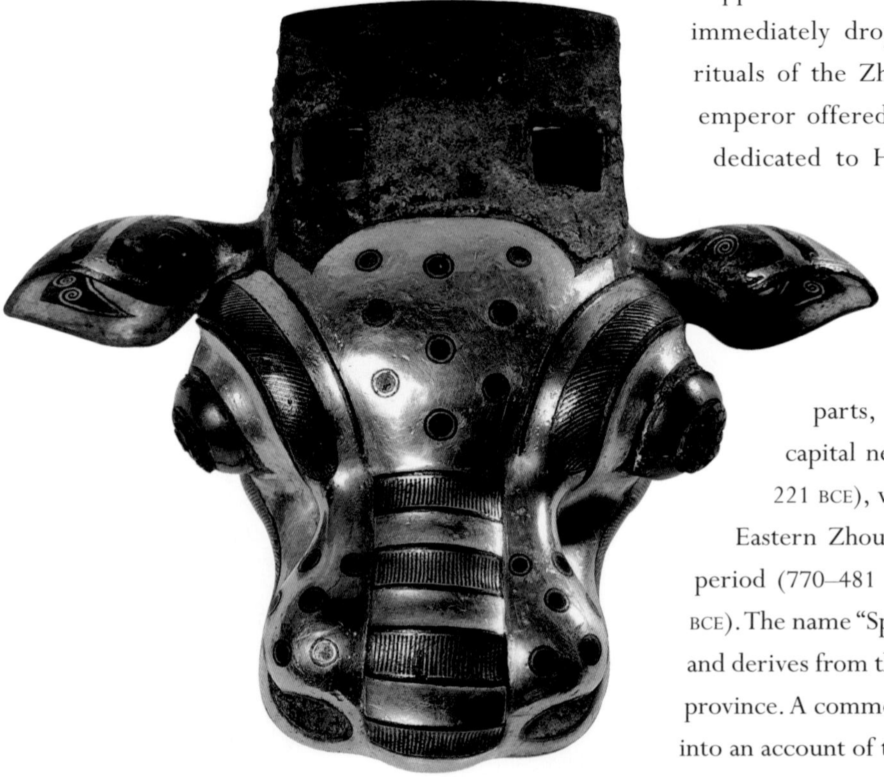

The Zhou were a tribe from what is now the region of Gansu and Shaanxi provinces in northwest China. These were horsebreeding areas and the Zhou may have benefited from their superior mobility. In about the mid-eleventh century BCE King Wu of Zhou conquered the last Shang king, Zhou Xin, and established a new dynasty with its capital near Xi'an in Shaanxi. Wu's brother, the duke of Zhou, consolidated the new dynasty. He also introduced rites and ritual music that later generations, influenced by Confucius (see page 24), regarded as emblematic of the virtue of the Zhou dynasty's founders.

The Zhou regime was always less centralized than the Shang. The king granted fiefdoms in different parts of his domains to branches of his own family, as well as to others whose ancestors had been close to the early Zhou kings.

To the Zhou people the most important deity was Heaven (Tian), worshipped as an overarching cosmic force. Shangdi was not immediately dropped but became even more remote. In the rituals of the Zhou and all subsequent dynasties, the king or emperor offered annual prayers for good harvests in temples dedicated to Heaven, of which the most famous surviving example is the Temple of Heaven in Beijing (see pages 158–161).

AN ERA OF CONFLICT

The Zhou dynasty is divided into two major parts, the Western Zhou (ca. 1050–770 BCE), with its capital near modern Xi'an, and the Eastern Zhou (770–221 BCE), when the capital was farther east at Luoyang. The Eastern Zhou is itself divided into the "Spring and Autumn" period (770–481 BCE) and the "Warring States" period (453–221 BCE). The name "Spring and Autumn" means something like "annals" and derives from the written annals of Lu, a small state in Shandong province. A commentary on these annals effectively expanded them into an account of the entire period.

LEFT
Chinese artisans produced inlay by the late Neolithic period (pre-1500 BCE), but it was not until the Eastern Zhou period, during the 5th or 4th century BCE, that bronze inlaid with gold and silver came into regular use. This lively, leaping feline is adorned with figures of stylized birds and snakes as well as abstract designs. It was probably made as a tray support. Inlaid animal figures were also made for use as table legs and corner fittings. Bronze with silver and gold inlay, Eastern Zhou period, 4th–3rd century BCE.

Over the course of the Spring and Autumn period the power of the Zhou kings declined as various feudal principalities asserted their *de facto* independence. As time went by the struggles of the feudal lords for supremacy became more bitter and the Zhou monarch was reduced to a mere titular head, whose function was mainly ceremonial.

During the Eastern Zhou the principalities nearer to the Zhou capital came to be called the "Central Country" (Zhongguo), a term—sometimes rendered "Middle Kingdom"—now used for the whole of China. But much larger principalities were growing in power, often measured by the number of chariots they possessed. To the north was Jin (in present-day Shanxi province), to the east Qi (in Shandong), and to the south Chu (in the middle reaches of the Yangzi). These states often fought each other, but sometimes struck up alliances, and at times, probably under duress, even recognized one of their number as their leader, or *ba*. Both Qi and Jin achieved this status during the seventh century BCE.

THE FLOWERING OF INTELLECT

The later Eastern Zhou period was known as the time of the Hundred Schools, a rather precise number that really indicates an unprecedented period of intellectual freedom and creativity, especially in the field of political and moral philosophy.

Toward the end of the Spring and Autumn period the small state of Lu was home to one of the greatest thinkers in Chinese history: Kongzi, or Kong Fuzi (Master Kong, 551–479 BCE), better known in the West as Confucius. The *Analects* (*Lunyu*), a compilation of his sayings, has been described as the most influential book in East Asia. Confucius inspired many contemporaries with his message that everyone should act in accordance with his or her place in the family and society, and be guided by *ren* (goodness, kindness) and *yi* (doing the right thing), rather than personal advantage. He deplored the breakdown of the old order that had led to the wars of his age and advocated a return to a society regulated by the rituals of the early Zhou kings, whom he revered.

Confucius failed to persuade the Chinese states of his own day to adopt his principles. Indeed, after his death, during the Warring States period, the wars and chaos he abhorred only intensified. However, members of the Confucian school, notably

BELOW
During the Eastern Zhou period prestigious weapons such as this double-edged sword were often adorned with precious metal and stones. The use of jade, which was associated with immortality, may have been intended to afford the bearer greater protection in combat. Bronze decorated with gold, turquoise, and jade. Eastern Zhou dynasty, 5th–3rd century BCE.

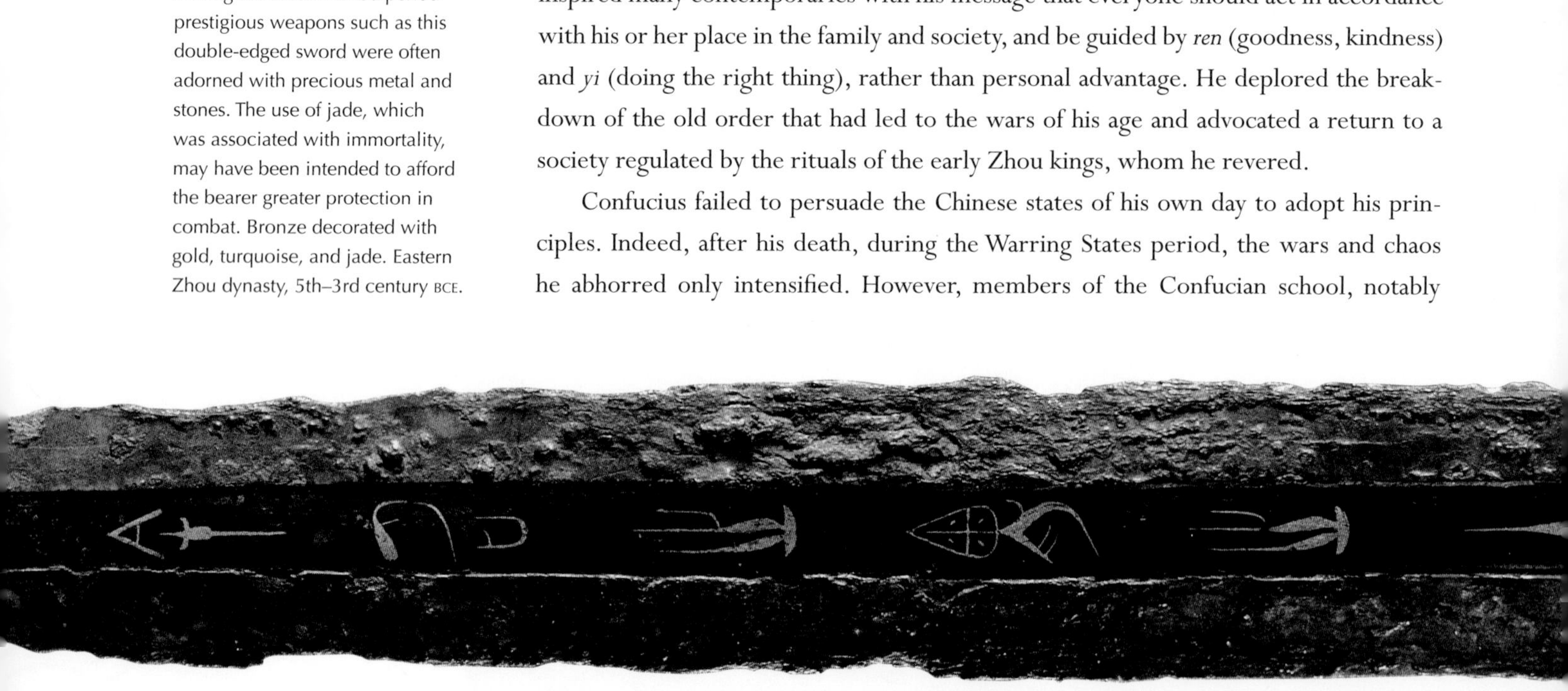

Mencius (Mengzi, 372–ca. 289 BCE) and Xunzi (ca. 310–215 BCE) continued his tradition. Mencius in particular carried on his mentor's missionary activity, haranguing rulers (in vain) to set an example of benevolence that would attract popular support to their regimes "as water flows downhill."

The school of Mozi, a military engineer who devised defense systems for states or cities, was in some ways even more idealistic. Mozi's recipe for peace was to abandon the restrictions imposed by status and to treat everyone with equal respect.

The third major school of philosophy to emerge was Daoism (Taoism), which developed from mystic cults and sorcery into a coherent moral philosophy during the Warring States period. Daoism's two major philosophers, Laozi ("Old Master") and Zhuangzi (Master Zhuang), rejected Confucian moralizing and the pursuit of power and wealth, advocating a simple life in harmony with nature. They believed that the ruler should not interfere in the lives of his subjects.

Quite the opposite view was taken by the Realist or Legalist school, which held that good order resulted from detailed laws rigidly enforced, with the demands of the state having priority over the individual. In the conditions of the time their policies seemed logical to the rulers of Qin, who adopted Legalism as their guiding philosophy.

The protracted wars of the later Eastern Zhou period undermined the traditional aristocracy because heavily ritualized warfare became anachronistic. Wars were no longer fought for honor but for territory. By the mid-third century BCE the number of states was reduced considerably, as one by one the smaller states fell victim to the larger. Eventually only seven remained. Six of them soon saw that their chief danger came from the state of Qin in the northwest, the original home of the Zhou people. In vain the states sought to form alliances against Qin, but they faced a formidable rival in King Zheng of Qin, who had succeeded in 247 BCE. One by one Zheng annexed the six states until the last remaining state, Wei, was defeated in 221 BCE and China was united.

ABOVE
An ornamental bronze plaque, inlaid with silver and gold, in the form of a fierce, open-mouthed tiger. King of Chinese beasts, the tiger symbolized a threat but was also associated with protection. Such dual meaning provided an ideal amulet motif, and tiger ornaments often accompanied the dead in the grave. Eastern Zhou, Warring States period, ca. 4th century BCE.

RITUAL BRONZES

Offerings to the Ancestors

At the heart of traditional Chinese popular beliefs is the idea that individuals continue to exist after death and are able to influence the fate of the living. During the Shang and Zhou dynasties, if not earlier, rulers and nobles seem to have given priority over all other activities to conducting ceremonies honoring their ancestors, and building an ancestral hall for this purpose took precedence over building palaces. Later documents of the Han dynasty show that the main hall, situated centrally in the north, was dedicated to the founding ancestor. This was never changed. The halls of subsequent generations were arranged in two north to south rows on either side, and could be substituted as time passed. Only the ruler could sacrifice to former kings. Other families sacrificed to their own family ancestors.

The ancestral rites involved great banquets to which the ancestor or ancestors themselves would be invited as guests of honor. To impress

BELOW
An elaborate ceremony, possibly an aristocratic ancestral rite, is depicted in this detail from a wine vessel. Figures are represented playing ritual bells similar to the one on the right. Bronze with copper inlay, Eastern Zhou period, ca. 500–350 BCE.

RIGHT
Ancestral rites involved the use of musical instruments such as this *zhong* (bell), decorated with dragons and bearing an inscription in a cartouche. It was suspended on a rope and struck. Bronze, Western Zhou period, ca. 9th–8th century BCE.

LEFT
One of a pair of ritual wine vessels or goblets known as *gu*, perhaps used to toast the dead at a ritual banquet for ancestors. The *gu* is decorated with the mysterious, stylized *taotie* motif. The vessel's curved profile, narrower at the waist, had been in use for ceramics since the earlier Erlitou era. Shang period, ca.1200 BCE.

them, the food would be served in the most precious vessels available. In Neolithic times these were of pottery but in the Shang and Zhou dynasties they were of bronze.

No exact record survives of the protocol that had to be observed at such ceremonies, but it was no doubt very elaborate and detailed. An account in *The Book of Songs* (*Shi Jing*, also translated as *The Classic of Poetry*), compiled in the Western Zhou period, includes the statement that "every custom and rite is observed and every smile and word is in place." A later account shows that even as simple a matter as serving wine to a guest was undertaken with great precision. The climax of the ceremony may well have been when the officiating priest ceremonially conveyed a message of greeting to the ancestor and returned with the ancestor's reply, thanking the descendant for the food and drink and for carrying out the rituals so correctly, and granting him many blessings.

This attention to detail provides some explanation as to why so many types of ritual bronze were made, both for preparing the food and drink and serving it. The gravity of the occasion ensured that no cost was spared in their production.

OPPOSITE
One of the standard vessels for dispensing food at ancestral rituals, the four-legged cauldron, or *fang ding*, derived its form, like other bronze ritual vessels, from earlier pottery of the Neolithic period, but its shape was too difficult to produce in ceramic. Bronze, Shang period, ca. 1500–1050 BCE.

MASTERWORKS IN METAL

Bronze vessels were cast with great skill in clay molds in sections that were then welded together. Some had pronounced flanges at the corners. They were of several main kinds: vessels for cooking, serving,and drinking, all with different names according to their uses and types. Some of the forms of the earliest vessels had clearly evolved from pottery prototypes, but they soon developed typical bronze characteristics. The most common form of decoration was a stylized animal mask called a *taotie*, with staring eyes. Which animal the *taotie* was based on is unclear but it later developed a body consisting of curvilinear patterns coiling round the vessel. Sometimes parts of the *taotie* would be modified into the shape of a dragon. Other animal motifs were also used, and occasionally human faces.

Although bronze technology did not develop significantly from Shang to Zhou, Zhou bronzes started to bear inscriptions on their inner surfaces indicating the occasion for which the bronze was cast, or recording the exploits of someone in battle. There was also increasing variety in their decoration, which sometimes included stylized birds and exotic animals from the south.

二

CHAPTER TWO

EPOCH OF EMPIRE

221 BCE–220 CE

THE QIN AND HAN

THE FIRST EMPEROR

The Qin Dynasty (221–206 BCE)

BELOW
The Great Wall at Gubeikou in Hebei province, 80 miles (130km) southeast of Beijing. Shihuangdi created the first rammed-earth "Long Wall" in the 3rd century BCE by connecting and extending existing northern frontier walls of the states he had conquered. The wall was rebuilt several times by later dynasties, notably the Ming, who fortified this stretch in 1567.

秦 During the last decade of the Warring States period, King Zheng of the state of Qin successively annexed the six other rival states, interned their aristocracy, and set up the first centrally governed, unified state in Chinese history. When the conquest of the rival states was complete, in 221 BCE, Zheng adopted the title Qin Shihuangdi, "the First Emperor of [the] Qin [dynasty]." Henceforth all the Chinese monarchs appended the honorific *huangdi* (emperor, literally "supreme ruler"). The name "China" itself derives from "Qin."

Shihuangdi fixed his capital at Xianyang, near modern Xi'an. One of his first moves, and a visible symbol of the unity he was determined to achieve, was to destroy the defensive frontier walls that had divided the recently annexed rival states.

However, he retained those walls that formed a boundary between the Chinese states and the nomads to the north, and in due course linked them together and extended them to form the first Great Wall of China.

ABOVE
This pair of bronze handles with animal faces adorned a funerary object and would therefore probably have had some protective symbolism. Late Qin or early Han dynasty, ca. 250–100 BCE.

UNITY AND REFORM

The political ideas that lay behind the new unified state had already been aired in Qin over a century before the conquest by a royal adviser, Shang Yang, or Lord Shang. In accordance with these ideas, Shihuangdi divided his domain into a system of prefectures and counties with governors appointed by him. He also built a network of roads and canals to link the many centers of population.

Under the guidance of his chief minister, Li Si, the emperor introduced further measures to make the new empire more difficult to unscramble. One of the most important of these was the unification of the Chinese script. During the period of interstate rivalry, some of the states had developed their own style of writing Chinese characters, which sometimes made them incomprehensible elsewhere. Qin Shihuangdi instructed his scribes to draw up an official list of characters written in a uniform style. This was modified in the following Han dynasty, but China has adhered to the principle of a unified script down to the present day. Shihuangdi also unified the currency. The states had produced metal coins that differed in shape, taking the forms of spades and

other tools. Under the Qin a unified bronze currency was minted, circular in shape with a square hole in the center (see illustration, left). This remained the standard form of Chinese coins right up to the twentieth century.

The emperor espoused the Legalist philosophy (see page 25), which favored practical action by the ruler, and banned all books except for those on medicine, agriculture, and divination. He also curtailed the activities of philosophical schools other than the Legalists; most notoriously, he burned the Confucian classics and buried alive a number of leading Confucian scholars.

In spite of his radical action against Confucianism, Shihuangdi carried his own belief in the afterlife to greater lengths than any other ruler in Chinese history, ordering the construction of a vast—and still largely unexcavated—mausoleum near Xi'an, guarded by an enormous army of terracotta warriors (see pages 36–41).

ABOVE
The *banliang* (half ounce) coin of Qin became the standard unit of currency following Qin's unification of China in 221 BCE. The round coin and square hole may reflect traditional belief in a circular heaven and square Earth. However, the hole may be purely functional. The coins were cast in molds and had to be filed after casting; by threading them onto a square rod, many could be filed at once. On either side of the hole are the characters *ban* (half, left) and *liang* (ounce). Bronze, state of Qin, 3rd century BCE.

THE FALL OF QIN

In order to carry out the emperor's colossal building projects, his officials conscripted hundreds of thousands of laborers. However, the punishments that applied to even minor offenses were so harsh that they triggered uprisings and assassination attempts. When the emperor died on a tour of eastern China in 210 BCE, Li Si kept his death a secret for fear of public unrest until the government had returned to Xianyang, where the emperor's eighteenth son, Huhai, was swiftly enthroned as Er Shihuangdi (Second Emperor, 210–206 BCE). As feared, Er Shi almost immediately faced a wave of uprisings. The biggest was led by a minor official named Liu Bang, who attacked and occupied Xianyang and overthrew the Qin dynasty in 206 BCE. For a time, China's new unity appeared to have been shattered.

OPPOSITE
A bronze mirror-back inlaid with warriors chasing feline creatures, from a Qin tomb at Shuihudi, Hebei province, Warring States period (453–221 BCE). At the center is a sacred mountain and the background pattern is a geometric cloud, perhaps representing the owner's desire for harmony with the cosmos and spiritual forces.

THE TERRACOTTA ARMY

A Force for the Afterlife

When in 210 BCE the chief minister Li Si secretly but successfully brought the body of Shihuangdi back to the capital Xianyang (see page 34) for burial, the mausoleum that the corpse was destined for had been under preparation for at least ten years. It lies under an artificial mound to the east of the modern city of Xi'an, not far from a hill called Lishan. The last resting place of the First Emperor—at the heart of what is effectively a gigantic necropolis complex—has never been opened and the Chinese authorities remain reluctant to excavate it fully until they are confident that conservation technology is sufficiently advanced to guarantee that whatever lies within the tomb will not be harmed in the process.

According to Sima Qian's *Historical Records*, written in the Han dynasty two centuries after the emperor's death, Shihuangdi recruited 700,000 men from all over China to work on the construction. They filled it with precious objects and the structure itself was characterized by ingenious devices. The emperor ordered crossbow traps to be set up so that any tomb robber who tried to get in would be shot. Inside the tomb—befitting a man who had conquered all opponents, forged a mighty, unified state, and had proclaimed his cosmic rulership—representations of the heavenly constellations shone from the ceiling and the regions of the Earth were reproduced on the floor. This Chinese microcosmos included all the country's main rivers, reproduced in mercury that was made to flow into a miniature ocean by mechanical means. Until the tomb is opened it will not be known exactly how much of Sima Qian's account is true—but scientists have recently detected traces of mercury in the nearby ground.

The rumored contents of the mausoleum and the existence of the burial pits (see below) containing an army for the afterlife may reflect the emperor's fears that the threat of death stalked him and that should he be unable to evade it he should be fully prepared and suitably equipped to extend his rule in the parallel spirit world.

RIGHT
Two views of the First Emperor's vast army of terracotta warriors in Pit no.1. Discovered in 1974 and covering an area roughly equivalent to two football fields the pit contained 6,000 life-sized figures, horses, and chariots in full battle array among the charred remains of the original roof, burned when the tomb complex was sacked within a few years of the emperor's death.

LEFT AND ABOVE

The First Emperor's terracotta troops were mass-produced using standard-sized molded parts for the basic figures. The torsos, limbs, and heads were manufactured separately and then assembled. To create the impression of a real army, the figures are of differing heights and postures (for example, standing infantrymen and crouching pikemen). Noses, ears, and hair were glued to the heads using a thick clay slip, and the face, hands, and hairstyle of each warrior were individually modeled. The entire basic figure was then covered in a layer of clay into which were sculpted details of uniforms and armor according to rank. After firing, the figures were painted realistically with lacquer-based paint, of which traces survive on some warriors, before being equipped with bronze weapons and arranged in their pits in battle formation.

BELOW
Close to the terracotta army was another pit containing nearly 90 suits of fishscale armor for soldiers and horses, along with more than 40 helmets and other accoutrements. The armor was manufactured from limestone plates joined with copper wire, apparently imitations of leather armor worn by the imperial army.

AN UNDERGROUND ARMY

Associated with the mausoleum are a number of large underground pits, the first of which was discovered in 1974 near Xi'an in Lintong county, Shaanxi province, by peasants looking for a place to dig a well. When archaeologists investigated the pits, they discovered nothing less than an entire army of life-size terracotta soldiers deployed in full battle array and prepared to guard the emperor in the afterlife. The troops, of which more than 8,000 have been uncovered so far, include officers and different kinds of warriors, such as cavalrymen, crossbowmen, and infantry armed with swords and

ABOVE
A bronze model of the emperor's carriage, complete with four exquisitely modeled horses that stand 2 ft. 4 in. (62 cm) high, and a coachman. The windows and doors, which open and close, bear decorative patterns including dragons and other figures. Thinner and more intricate than typical earlier bronzes, the model was cast using advanced techniques of bronze casting and assembly.

pikes. The bodies of the soldiers, many wearing intricately reproduced fishscale armor, were made of standard parts but their faces were all individual and probably modeled either from life or from portraits of real men. An examination has shown that the warriors were made with clay from the nearby Lishan hill. The Qin craftsmen solved the problem of creating stable freestanding clay figures by making the bodies and arms hollow and the legs solid. After the bodies and heads had been mass-produced they were joined together with strips of clay, before the facial and other features, such as the often elaborate hairstyles, were carved and molded. Finally, the assembled figures were fired at a high temperature and painted.

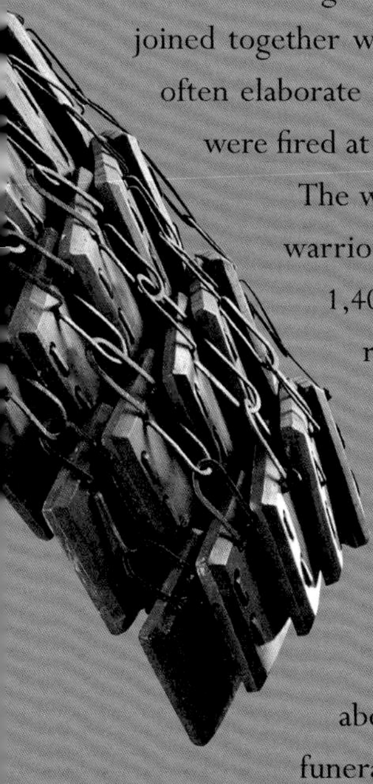

The warrior pits were 16 ft. (5 m) deep and the largest, containing 6,000 warriors and horses, measured 4 acres (1.6 ha). A second pit housed 1,400 figures and a third contained the command unit with high-ranking officers, junior officers, and a chariot drawn by four horses. The floors of the pits were tiled with bricks and the pits themselves were originally roofed over in wood, much of which was burned when rebel armies sacked the imperial tomb and its associated buildings at the fall of the Qin dynasty. Many of the figures were smashed but have now been painstakingly pieced together.

Also discovered were the remains of a number of small buildings above ground, perhaps for receiving officials supervising the emperor's funeral rites, together with a number of smaller pits, one of which had in it a bronze replica of the emperor's chariot. No expense was spared in reproducing the smallest details. In other pits real horses were buried and coffins containing exotic animals from the emperor's personal menagerie.

汉

THE MANDATE OF HEAVEN

The Western Han Dynasty, 206 BCE–8 CE

汉 Within four years of defeating the Qin army under the Second Emperor in 206 BCE, Liu Bang had eliminated his main rival among the rebel leaders and established his capital at Chang'an (modern Xi'an). This marked the beginning of the Han dynasty, which ruled China for nearly four hundred years (206 BCE–185 CE), though like the Zhou dynasty it was divided into two periods, the Western Han and Eastern Han.

Liu Bang reaffirmed Chinese unity by continuing many of the institutions introduced by the First Emperor, including the division of his territory into prefectures and counties. The Han dynasty later strengthened the state by introducing a uniform tax system, which was achieved by compiling detailed population censuses that historians consider to be as accurate as any taken in later ages.

In contrast to the Qin, the Han emperor granted fiefs to some of those who had helped him conquer the Qin, and also to members of the royal family. These fiefs

BELOW
The burial suit and bronze headrest of Princess Dou Wan (died ca. 100 BCE), wife of the Western Han prince Liu Sheng (died 114 BCE), who was buried in a similar suit of jade plates joined together with gold wire. Jade was believed to preserve the body after death. Discovered in Mancheng county, Hebei, in 1968, the royal couple's undisturbed tombs contained a wealth of precious artifacts.

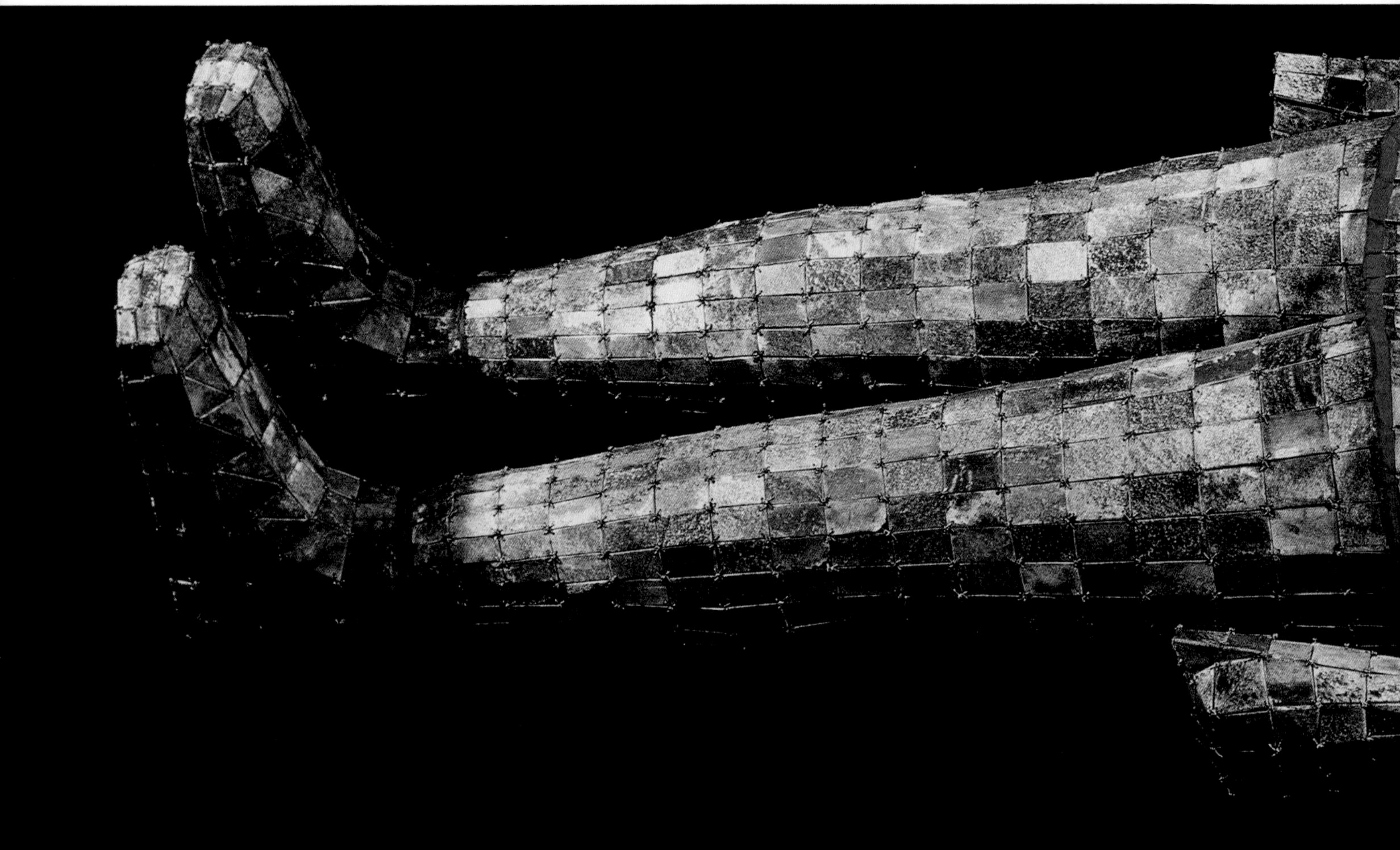

covered most of his territory, but their administration was still supervised by imperial officials, and the lords who held the fiefdoms were not allowed to gain the sort of power achieved by the principalities of the Eastern Zhou. All the same, they did become a threat to the dynasty forty years later and the Han emperors sought to curb their power. Emperor Wu Di (ruled 141–87 BCE) instituted measures to break the fiefholders' grasp on their territories by decreeing that their land had to be divided equally among their sons and not just bequeathed to one sole heir.

Some of the harshest laws of the Qin were repealed, including the banning of non-Legalist books. Indeed, Wu Di went further and espoused Confucianism as the state ideology, proscribing non-Confucian schools of thought. From then on Confucianism held a predominant position in China, and the Confucian classics became the basis of Chinese education down to the end of the imperial age.

The Han established state monopolies over the salt and iron industries as a means of stabilizing the national finances and providing funds to fight the tribes that threatened China's northern frontiers (a liquor monopoly was also proposed but this idea was abandoned as unworkable). The state duly established forty-eight iron foundries

ABOVE
A *zun* (wine jug) from Xinping county, Shaanxi province, made in the form of a rhinoceros and inlaid with cloud motifs. Bronze with gold and silver inlay, Western Han dynasty, 2nd–1st century BCE.

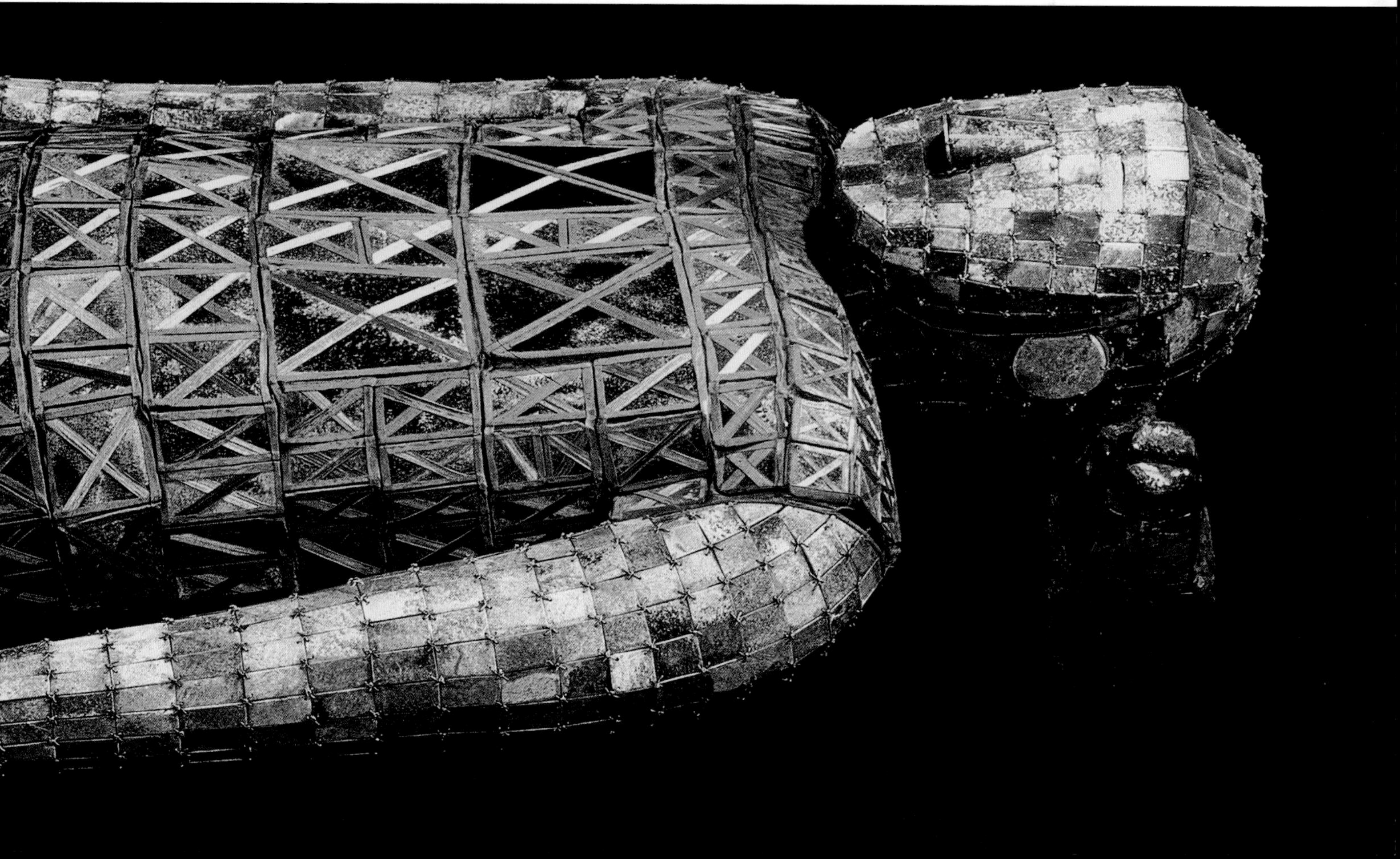

employing many thousands of workers. For other industries outside the monopoly, such as silkweaving and lacquerware, rich merchants set up hundreds of workshops. The monopoly lasted for a hundred years, but even before it ended the state had set up its own workshops for producing luxury silks, while private iron foundries had also started to flourish.

EXPANSION IN ASIA

On the collapse of the Qin, an array of northern nomadic tribes known as the Xiongnu were forming a confederation that became a growing threat to the state. Chinese dynasties adopted two different policies to deal with this menace. When the empire was relatively weak, they attempted to buy the nomads off with gifts of silks, alcohol, rice, and so on, or perhaps by presenting a Chinese royal bride to a nomad ruler, as happened in 198 BCE. This event is still remembered in Chinese drama and storytelling.

However, when the Chinese felt strong enough, they would launch military expeditions to control the tribes' home territories. To this end, the Han sent expeditions

BELOW
A peacock, a dragon, and a tiger decorate this elaborate harness frontlet (*danglu*), which originally would have hung down between the eyes of a horse. Bronze and gold leaf, Western Han dynasty, ca. 1st century BCE.

into Central Asia to contact a people called the Yue Zhi, known in the West as Indo-Scythians, who were old enemies of the Xiongnu.

In 127 BCE the Han launched an offensive against the Xiongnu, which within twelve years had removed their threat from the north. Following the Han expeditions, many thousands of Chinese were settled in the northwest on the borders of the Xiongnu territories. Many were both farmers and soldiers, ready to be mobilized if hostilities threatened, but tilling the soil in times of peace.

The Han went on to consolidate their presence in Central Asia. They did not establish direct rule there, but set up garrisons at key points on important silk routes and became the dominant influence in the whole region. In addition to Central Asia, the Han also expanded their trade and influence toward Manchuria and Korea in the northeast, and toward the borders of Vietnam and Burma in the southwest.

RICHES FOR THE DEAD: HAN ARTS

Most of what is known about artistic development during the Han dynasty is derived from grave goods obtained from excavated tombs. During the Han there were changes in the Chinese attitude toward burials, which led to an increase in both the number

RIGHT
A silk funeral banner from the tomb of Lady Dai (died ca. 166 BCE) at Mawangdui in Changsha, Hunan. It probably represents the universe, with an underworld (bottom), the surface of the Earth (center), and the heavens (top). Lady Dai is shown in the middle of the lower section, two women kneeling before her.

ABOVE
By the Western Han dynasty lacquerware had developed into a colorful and highly skilled art form, and lacquered wooden dishes, bowls, and other goods were much prized. Decoration ranged from energetic swirling scroll patterns, as on this dish, to both real and fabulous creatures. Western Han dynasty, 2nd–1st century BCE.

and nature of such artifacts. It was no longer thought necessary to place precious bronze articles in tombs; less costly earthenware or wood models represented the deceased's needs in the afterlife. Such objects were already found in tombs of the Warring States period, but they reached a higher level of importance and artistic excellence in the Han. The multiplicity of such objects recovered from Han tombs include pottery figurines of servants, musicians, entertainers, animals, and copies of everyday objects.

The Chinese of the Han dynasty had no religious authority to pronounce on the nature of the afterlife, and so their tombs sometimes reflected different ideas on the subject. By the early Han, a figure named Huang Di, the Yellow Emperor, was thought to rule the spirit world, including all the other deities. He governed the five sacred mountains, chief of which was Mount Tai in Shandong province. From this time onward grave goods included such objects as incense burners in the shape of mountains (see page 53).

AN ARISTOCRATIC AFTERLIFE

Dating from the mid-second century BCE, the tomb of the aristocratic Lady Dai at Mawangdui near Changsha, Hunan province, has yielded an astonishing quantity of grave goods, including extremely fine embroidered and printed silks—some bearing designs symbolizing longevity—as well as a large amount of lacquerware and other articles, such as documents. There is even a map of the area of southern China where the grave is situated. Dai's tomb has a capacious outer coffin with three inner coffins containing artifacts representing four different possible abodes of the dead. One of these is the universe, with its heavenly bodies, such as the sun, moon, and earth, including a picture of Lady Dai herself on a silk banner (see illustration, page 45). The underworld and the abode of the immortals (the nearest to the Western idea of heaven) are also represented.

There is also a house with four chambers mimicking the deceased's earthly residence, complete with furnishings and figurines of servants, musicians, and dancers. Dai's body was astonishingly well preserved, owing to the tightly sealed coffins, buried deep underground under layers of charcoal and clay, and perhaps also to the fact that she had ingested lead, mercury, arsenic, and cinnabar over a considerable period, probably as a means of bodily preservation.

Other lavishly furnished Western Han tombs are those of Prince Liu Sheng and his consort Dou Wan, discovered at Mancheng in Hebei province, northern China. Unlike the Mawangdui tomb, these were hollowed out of solid rock at the end of a long tunnel into a mountain. They are most famous for the burial suits in which their two occupants were dressed, made of small jade plaques, pierced at the corners and sewn together with gold wire (see illustration, pages 42–43). The plaques were not made of nephrite, but they were still classed as jade, which was thought to guarantee eternal life (or, in this case, afterlife).

BELOW
In 109 BCE the Han emperor Wu Di subjugated the kingdom of Dian in present-day Yunnan province. This container for cowrie shells, which the Dian used as currency, depicts a battle between Dian warriors and nomads. Bronze, from a tomb at Lijiashan, Jiang-chuan county, Yunnan, Western Han dynasty, 2nd–1st century BCE.

A COSMOPOLITAN EMPIRE

The Eastern Han Dynasty (25–220 CE)

BELOW
A masterwork of Han sculpture, this statue (13.5 in/34.5 cm high) of a galloping horse poised on the back of a swallow was found in a tomb in Wuwei county, Gansu province, in 1969. The sculptor has accurately depicted the legs of a horse at full gallop—a hugely difficult feat of observation for the naked eye. Bronze, Eastern Han dynasty, 25–220 CE.

In 8 CE the Han dynasty was overthrown by the rebel Wang Mang, who set up the short-lived Xin dynasty. However, a member of the Han royal family succeeded in restoring the Han in 25 CE, based at Luoyang, a new capital farther east. This marks the start of the Eastern Han dynasty.

At the outset the Eastern Han continued to prosper economically, and culturally it was a period of remarkable innovation. The first paper had been invented in China around two centuries earlier, but an imperial eunuch, Cai Lun (ca. 50–121 CE), achieved fame by manufacturing a paper of greatly improved quality in the workshops of Emperor He Di (ruled 88–106 CE). For writing, paper henceforth came to replace the rather clumsy and heavy scrolls made of slips of wood or bamboo strung together lengthways, as well as the prohibitively expensive silk. Other inventions of the Eastern Han included the world's first seismograph, while Eastern Han astronomers were the

first to record sunspots and supernovae. Water power was widely used, for example to operate bellows in iron smelting. In medicine, acupuncture was being practiced by this time, and the Eastern Han physician Hua Tuo was the first surgeon to anesthetize his patients (with wine mixed with various herbs) for major operations.

A HUNDRED FLOWERS: THINKERS AND WRITERS

During the Eastern Han there was a resurgence of intellectual and literary activity to rival the intellectual explosion of the Eastern Zhou. It included philosophical speculation and a re-examination of the ancient classic texts. A dispute that was to last for

ABOVE
A relief of Xiwang Mu, "Queen Mother of the West," the highest goddess in the Daoist pantheon and the guardian of the secret of immortality. One of her familiars, the toad of immortality, squats at her feet. Decorated brick from a tomb in Xindu county, Sichuan. Eastern Han dynasty, 25–220 CE.

RIGHT
Remarkably accurate and detailed pottery models made as grave goods during the later Han dynasty constitute one of the few extant sources of information on Chinese architecture before the Tang dynasty. This model of a five-story building, perhaps a grain silo, already displays the typical Chinese construction of tiled roofs supported on elaborate brackets. Painted pottery, Eastern Han dynasty, 2nd century CE.

many centuries arose from the supposed discovery of books that had been walled up in Confucius's house in Lu during the proscriptions of the Qin dynasty. Written in the ancient pre-Han script, these were enthusiastically supported by some Han dynasty scholars, who hailed them as the authentic versions of the classics. Others, however, preferred the reconstructions of the classics by later writers.

One of the outstanding intellectuals of the Eastern Han was Wang Chong (27–97 CE), whose *Discourses* broke fresh ground in philosophical speculation. He departed from fashionable modes of thought and showed a rationalist interest in the natural sciences such as physics, biology, and even genetics. Basing his arguments on experience and observable reality, he rejected the widespread idea of the afterlife out of hand and declared that the mind and the senses cannot depart without the body. He also rejected the popular belief in Fate.

Wang Chong lived in a time of relative optimism, but this did not extend beyond the early years of the Eastern Han. Toward the end of the dynasty economic and political crises led to a return to the traditions of the Warring States and the philosophical schools of Laozi, Zhuangzi, and even Legalism. Classical studies and Confucianism were already in decline by this time.

While Confucianism remained the state orthodoxy, it was during this period that Buddhist monks from India and Central Asia started to build temples in China, the first being the White Horse monastery near Luoyang, which according to tradition was built in the reign of the second Eastern Han emperor, Ming Di (ruled 57–75 CE). The first Buddhist texts were translated into Chinese at this time (see also pages 66–73).

The Han Dynasty's political and military control of Central Asia greatly facilitated the spread of Buddhism eastward as well as bringing wealth to traders both in Central Asia and in China itself. But this control demanded continued vigilance. One of China's national heroes of the period was the soldier–diplomat Ban Chao (32–102 CE), a man of humble origins who quickly rose to a position of trust through talent and personality. He was despatched westward more than once to use his

BELOW
This model may portray a type of jester who spoke or sang stories in time to his own rhythmic accompaniment on the drum. The figure is apparently a dwarf, like Zhan, who was court jester of the emperor Qin Shihuangdi and is mentioned in the writings of the Han historian Sima Qian. Painted pottery, from Xindu county, Sichuan. Eastern Han dynasty, 1st–3rd century CE.

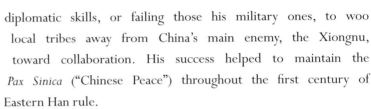

diplomatic skills, or failing those his military ones, to woo local tribes away from China's main enemy, the Xiongnu, toward collaboration. His success helped to maintain the *Pax Sinica* ("Chinese Peace") throughout the first century of Eastern Han rule.

During the second century CE the stability of the Han regime came under threat from the machinations of powerful landlords. The situation in the imperial palace deteriorated as the families of the royal in-laws started to wield power, and the clique of palace eunuchs became a serious threat to the dynasty. Matters were made worse by a succession of child emperors, which meant a lack of strong central authority. All these troubles led to heavier taxation of the peasants as a means of acquiring money for increasingly unstable governments.

DECLINE AND FALL

Toward the end of the second century unrest grew. In 185 CE a secret sect called the Yellow Turbans, purporting to be followers of the true path (*dao*), launched a large-scale rebellion, which seriously damaged the Han dynasty and ultimately led to the fragmentation of the country and the downfall of the dynasty. In 220 CE the last Han emperor, Xian Di, was forced to abdicate, ushering in a long period of political disunion.

Like all dynasties, the Han met an ignominious end, but it was nonetheless the longest reigning dynasty in Chinese history. China has always been a land of many nationalities, but by far the largest, now well over ninety percent of the population, who might be described as ethnic Chinese, have referred to themselves as the "Han" since the time of the dynasty.

It was also during the Han that the tradition of recording historical events and the activities of emperors and princes, which had become well established before the Han, was consolidated into a regulated activity of Chinese governments. The model for the official histories of all the subsequent dynasties down to the Ming was the *Historical Records* compiled by Sima Qian (ca. 135–93 BCE). This history of over half a million words was divided into separate sections: annals, chronological tables, chapters on various topics, and biographies of eminent men. Unlike the subsequent dynastic histories, it covered almost 3,000 years from the earliest times to the Western Han.

In the Eastern Han the scholar Ban Gu (32–92 CE), worked on an unofficial history of the Western Han begun by his father and based on Sima Qian's model. Ban Gu was reported and imprisoned, but the emperor read and approved his work and he was allowed to continue. This was the first of China's official dynastic histories.

EASTERN HAN ARTS

Grave goods continued to feature in the artistic heritage of the Eastern Han. Some display a very high level of modeling skills and artistic refinement, as displayed in the lively earthenware figurine of a squatting ballad-singer with a drum, unearthed in a tomb at Majiashan in Sichuan, West China. Another expressive earthenware figure from a Sichuan tomb, her face and posture full of character, is a kneeling woman holding a fan. In addition to human figures, there were pottery models of towers, ponds, farm animals, and dwellings; like the human figures, some of these still bear signs of pigmentation.

A tomb at Cangshan, Shandong province, contains a series of relief carvings depicting a funeral procession, which is crossing a bridge to the gate of the otherworld, resembling the door of a country inn. The deceased is then entertained at a banquet where he enjoys some musical entertainment. The final carving shows him driving a chariot in the country with his companions. The reliefs depict some elements of the afterlife, which, while ideas about its details varied, from the Han dynasty onward was expected to be harmonious and guided by Confucian concepts of morality.

RIGHT
Boshanlu, incense burners that represent Mount Bo (Boshan), the mythical mountain home of the Immortals in the Eastern Sea, first appeared in the Qin and Han dynasties. Smoke rising from holes in the lid would create an image of mist or cloud wreathing the mountain. Gilt bronze, Han dynasty, 3rd century BCE.

OPPOSITE
"Money trees" are named for the square-holed coins growing among their delicately cast branches. Also in the tree are various figures and animals associated with immortality: together with the coins, these were believed to aid the deceased on his or her journey to the afterlife. Ceramic and bronze, from Pengshan county, Sichuan. Eastern Han dynasty, 1st–3rd century CE.

三

CHAPTER THREE

RIVALS FOR POWER

220–581 CE

THE PERIOD OF DISUNION

魏

CLANS AND KINGDOMS

The Three Kingdoms and the Jin, 220–316 CE

The four centuries of disunion that followed the collapse of the Han dynasty was accompanied by the gradual incursion of non-Chinese nomadic peoples into the country from the north and northwest. But first came a period of seemingly endless civil wars, which began in the last years of the Han. Eventually a Han military leader Cao Cao (Ts'ao Ts'ao), who was not an aristocrat but the adopted son of a palace eunuch, beat his rivals in North China and set up the kingdom of Wei, with Luoyang as its capital. In 208 Cao Cao marched on the south in an attempt to reunify the fragmenting empire, but his huge army was defeated at the Battle of the Red Cliffs by an alliance of two rival warlords, Liu Bei and Sun Quan.

Nevertheless, Wei flourished under Cao Cao's rule as a result of his economic policies. These included the establishment of agricultural colonies to support his armies, some numbering tens of thousands of men, many of them impoverished peasants. The hired farmers had to give a large proportion of their produce to the military, but in return they had stable employment and guaranteed protection in time of war.

Cao Cao died in 220, and a few months later his son Cao Pi dethroned the last Han emperor. This marks the start of the period of the Three Kingdoms (which is some-

BELOW

Special Envoys, a Song-dynasty copy of a scroll painting by Xiao Yi (508–554), the son of the emperor Wu of Liang, one of China's numerous regional dynasties during the Period of Disunion. The painting depicts envoys from various foreign states, alongside an inscription describing each country and its relations with China.

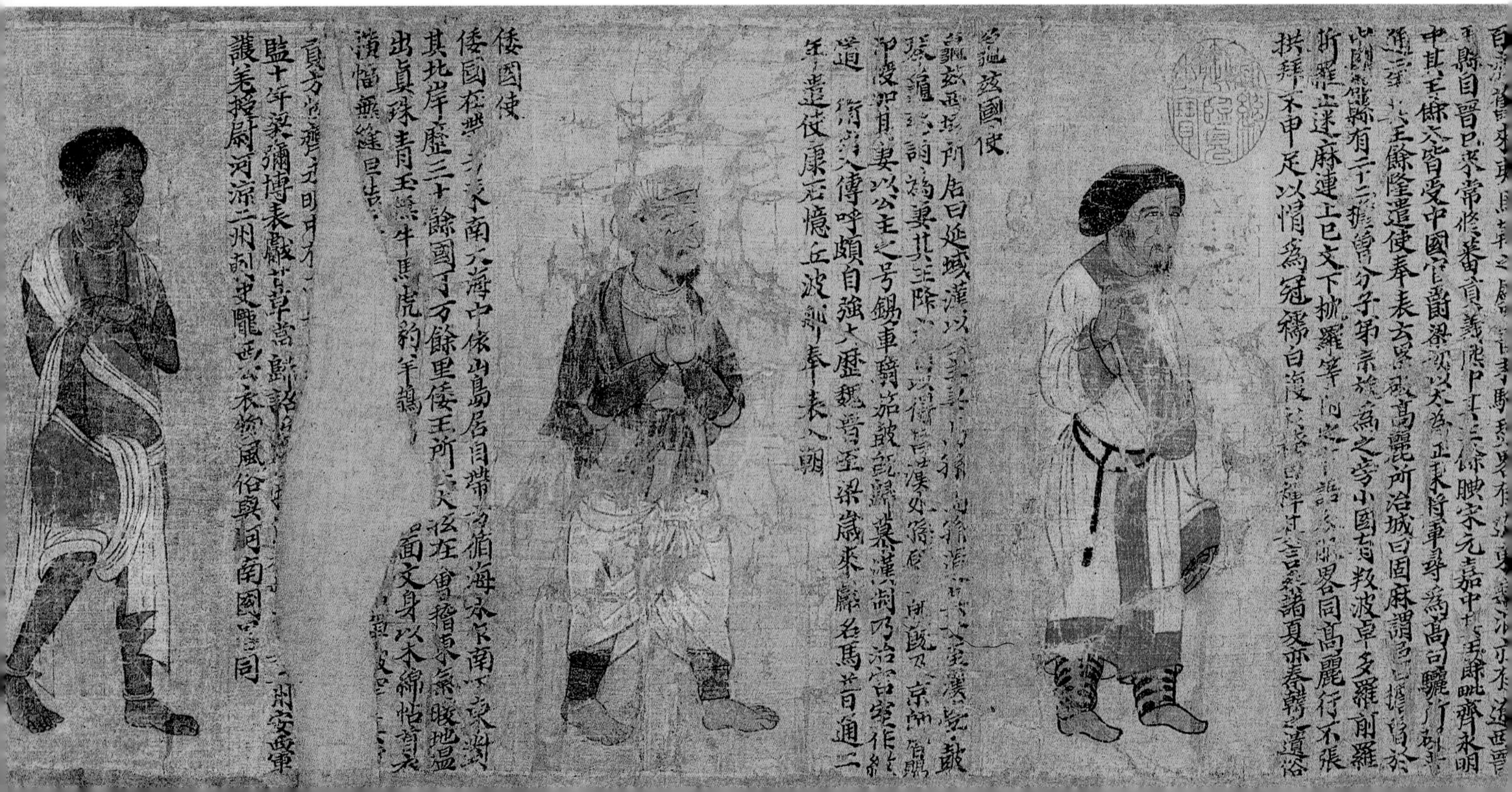

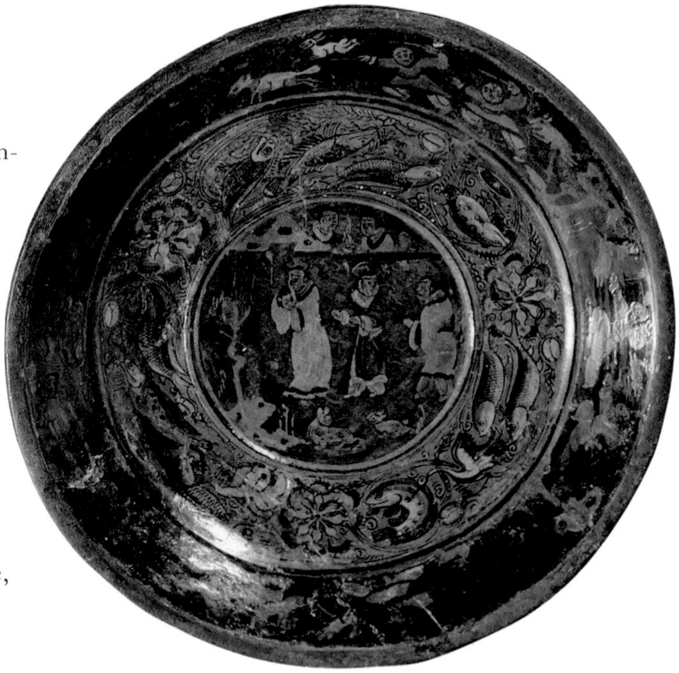

thing of a misnomer, since the rulers of all three states styled themselves emperors). Cao Pi gave his father the posthumous title Emperor Wu of Wei.

Liu Bei, a member of the ruling family of the defunct Han dynasty, presided over a separate kingdom based in Chengdu in Sichuan in West China. In 221 he declared himself emperor and called his kingdom the Han, in an attempt to continue the dynasty, but it came to be known as Shu, an old name for Sichuan. The third kingdom was founded by the southern warlord Sun Quan, who declared himself emperor of (Eastern) Wu, based first at Wuhan on the Yangzi River and later at Jianye, present-day Nanjing.

HISTORY AND ROMANCE

What is known of the Three Kingdoms comes mainly from the historical records and other writings of the time. But most Chinese are familiar with the main characters involved in the three states' frequent wars owing to the lasting popularity of the first of China's classical works of fiction, *The Romance of the Three Kingdoms*, written much later (see page 170). Episodes from it are frequently played on the stage or recounted by storytellers, and such characters as Cao Cao, Liu Bei, the cunning strategist Zhuge

ABOVE
A lacquered plate from the tomb of General Zhu Ran (182–248), commander of the army of Wu under Sun Quan. The tomb was discovered in 1984 in Ma'anshan, Anhui province. Three Kingdoms period.

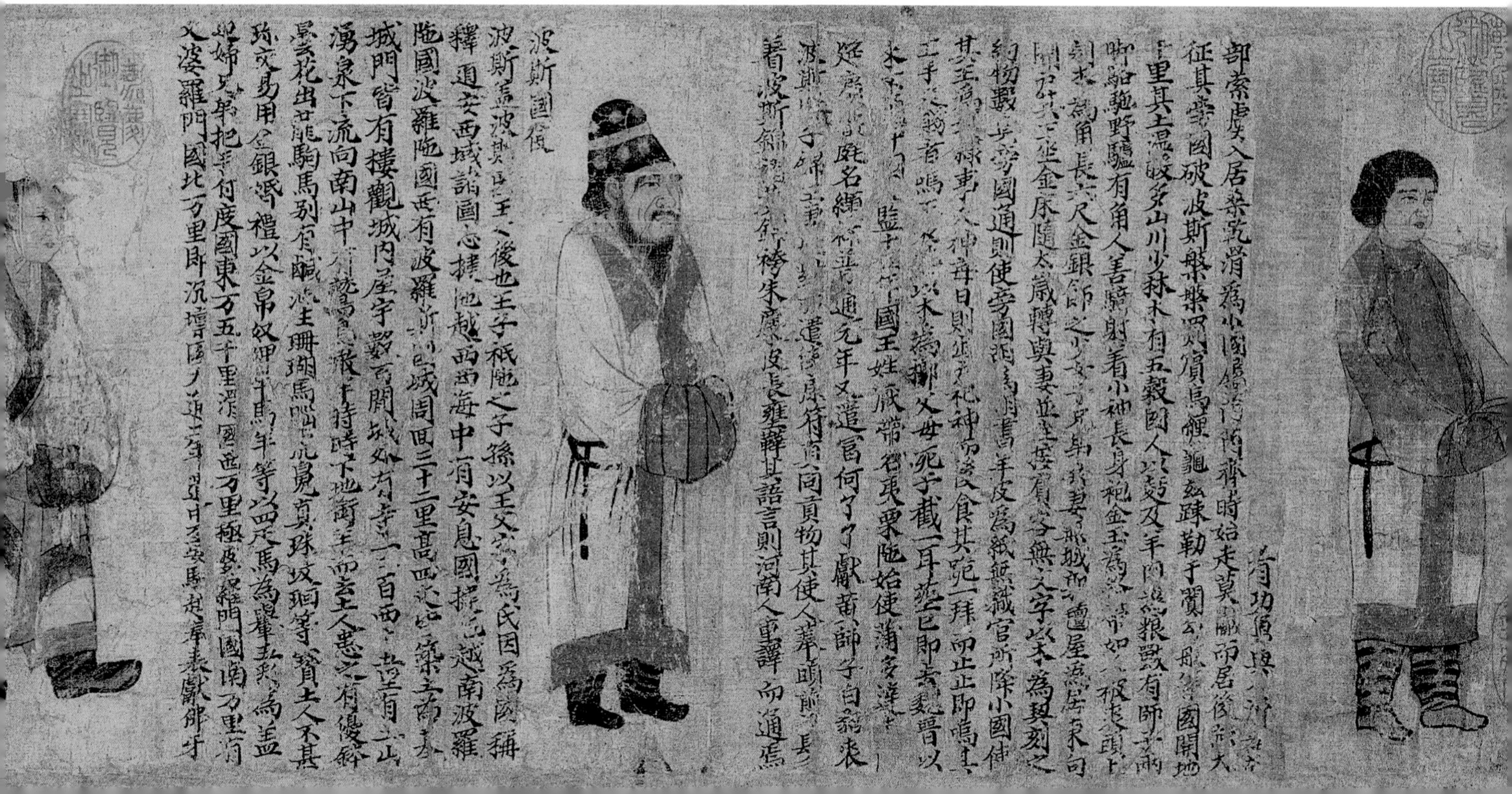

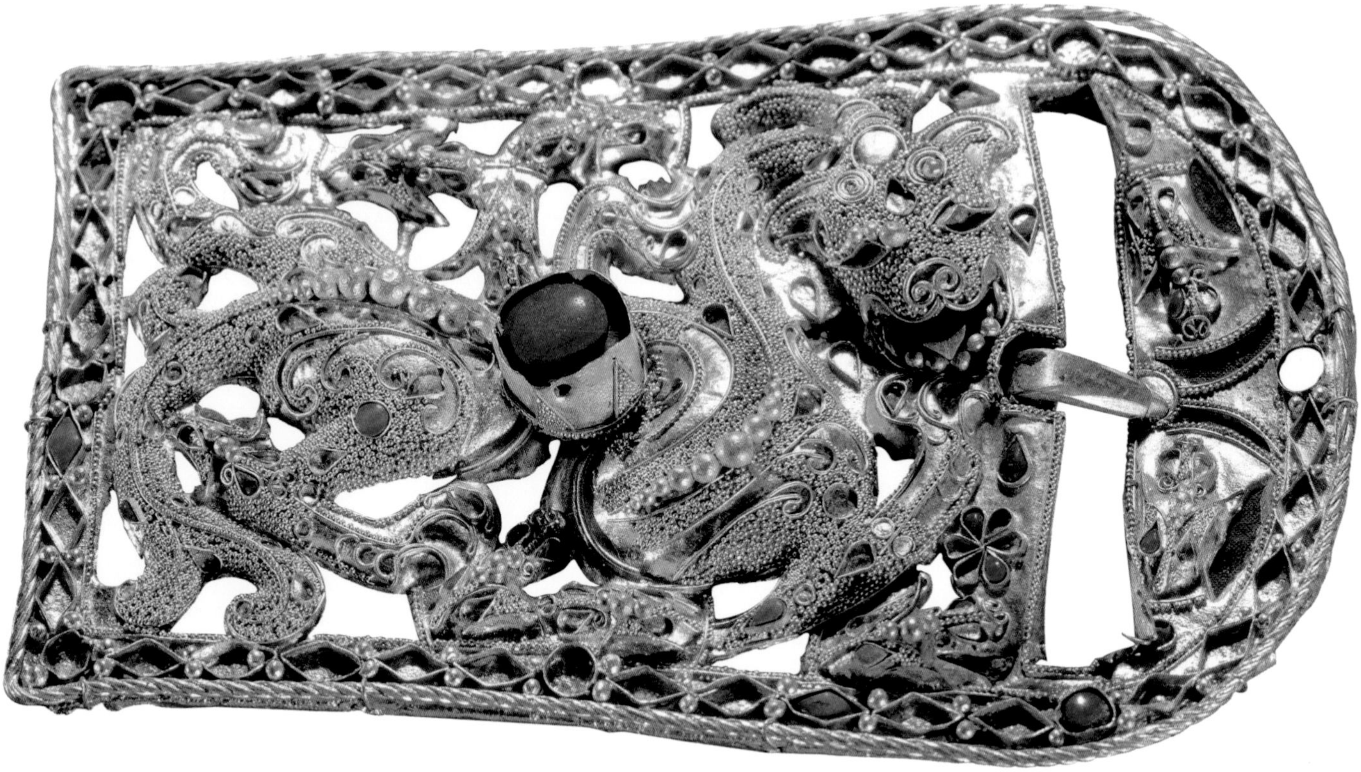

ABOVE
A gold belt buckle with a dragon design, discovered in the tomb of Liu Hong in Anxiang county, Hunan. Western Jin dynasty, 265–316 CE. Several of the metalworking techniques used in its manufacture, such as filigree and granulation, are of Central Asian origin, but the dragon motif is strongly Chinese.

Liang, and the brave and loyal warrior Guan Yu are household names. Guan Yu has even attained the status of a god in Chinese popular religion. Like most historical fiction, *The Romance* takes some liberties with the facts for the sake of a good story. For example, in the book, Zhu Ran, the commander of the armies of Wu, is killed by the hero Zhao Yun, head of the army of Shu, in 222. In reality Zhu Ran died in 248, some years after his rival. His tomb was discovered to great acclaim as recently as 1984 in Ma'anshan, Anhui province. The highest-status tomb of the period so far excavated, it revealed a wealth of artifacts, including clothing and fine painted lacquerware (see page 57).

THE WESTERN JIN

The great clans jostling for power toward the end of the Three Kingdoms period included the Sima family in the kingdom of Wei. In 263 Sima Yan, prince of Jin, conquered the kingdom of Shu for Wei. In 265 he forced the emperor of Wei to abdicate and established the Jin dynasty (265–420). Like the Zhou and the Han, this dynasty falls into two eras, the Western Jin (265–316) based at Luoyang, and Eastern Jin (317–420) based in present-day Nanjing (see pages 60–61). Sima Yan (or Emperor Wu of Jin, ruled 265–290) immediately set out to consolidate his rule. To this end he created seventeen fiefdoms with his relatives in charge. His ambition was to unify the whole of China under the Jin, and he put into effect vigorous measures to that end, including a new legal code, new land regulations, measures to curb the power of other families, and military expeditions against the southern kingdom of Wu.

Although the Jin succeeded in defeating Wu in 280, reuniting China briefly, the dynasty's policies came unstuck ten years later, after the death of Sima Yan. The cause was rivalry among the great noble families, some of whom had married into the Sima. The first to cause trouble was Sima's widow Empress Jia, whose own family gradually began to gain the ascendancy. This infuriated some of the Sima princes, and the last decade of the third century was occupied by the War of the Eight Princes in which the Sima family fought back against the Jia. But their eventual victory brought no real peace and left the Jin state weak and vulnerable to attack from the northern "barbarians."

In 308, Liu Cong, a noble of the nomadic Xiongnu people in the north, which had been growing in strength in the face of Jin weakness, set up the first of a succession of non-Chinese-controlled states known as the Northern Dynasties. (However, whether they were Tibetans or Tanguts from Central Asia, or Turks, Mongolians, and Tanguts of the northern steppes, these peoples had already absorbed much of Chinese culture as well as many Chinese political practices and concepts. As time went by, intermarriage between the native majority and the incoming "barbarians" was so common that their ethnic identity became blurred.)

Liu Cong's family had assumed the Chinese surname Liu, the same as that borne by the Han dynasty, and Liu Cong claimed his state, which he called Han Zhao (304–319), to be the rightful successor to the Han empire. In 316 the Jin emperor surrendered to Liu Cong, ending Western Jin rule and inaugurating the period of China's greatest disunity, with the north and south being ruled for the following two and a half centuries by a sometimes bewildering succession of regimes.

BELOW
A pair of woven shoes found in a tomb in Turfan, Xinjiang Uighur Autonomous Region. They bear Chinese characters for "marquis" and "prince" and "rich and noble," and indicate the extent of Chinese cultural influence among neighboring peoples in the Period of Disunion. Eastern Jin dynasty, 4th century.

晋

FIEFDOMS AND WARLORDS

The Northern and Southern Dynasties (317—581 CE)

OPPOSITE
Bird and animal designs adorn this dark blue and red brocade discovered in a tomb at Astana, near Turfan, Xinjiang. Northern and Southern Dynasties period, ca. 5th century.

BELOW
Two naturalistic, 6th-century gilt-bronze peacock plaques, 2.5 in. (6.3 cm) wide. A Chinese symbol of beauty and dignity, the peacock was a popular feminine motif.

晋 Following the fall of the Western Jin dynasty in the north, in 317 a Jin prince and remnants of the court established a new regime in the south at Jiankang (present-day Nanjing), which is known as the Eastern Jin (317–420) and was essentially a coalition of powerful aristocratic families. This initiated the Northern and Southern Dynasties era of the Period of Disunion, which lasted until the end of the sixth century and marked the low point of imperial power and the high point of aristocratic influence. The unrest stemming from the Xiongnu invasions of the north caused a flood of refugees to the south that was at first a problem for the Eastern Jin, but in time the incomers' skills added to the economic advances that the south had started to make. Soon the Eastern Jin overran Sichuan, opening avenues of trade with Central and South Asia and boosting the dynasty's prosperity before its overthrow by the Liu Song (420–479).

Contemporary with the Eastern Jin and the four dynasties that succeeded them in the south (Liu Song, Southern Qi, Liang, and Chen), the north was parceled up among a succession of short-lived "barbarian" regimes known as the Sixteen Kingdoms. In 383

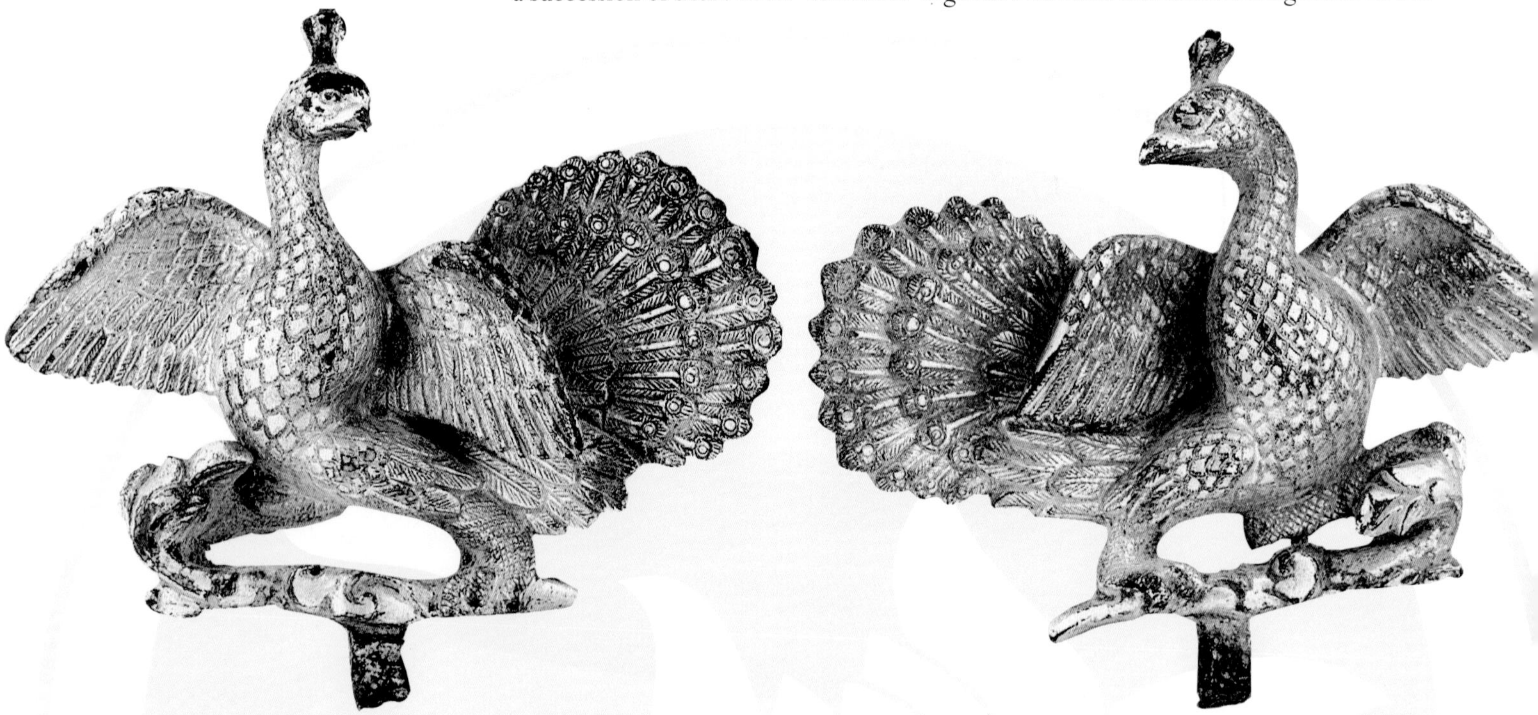

at the Fei River, in one of the decisive battles in Chinese history the south beat off a determined effort by the north to unify China. The two regions remained at loggerheads for nearly two centuries more, with conflict interspersed with short interludes of peace when the economy briefly recovered.

OPPOSITE
The grapevine motifs and form of this stem cup from Pingcheng (present-day Datong, Shanxi province), the first Northern Wei capital, derive ultimately from Greco-Roman examples, possibly via the Indo-Hellenistic cultures of what is now Afghanistan. Gilt bronze, Northern Wei dynasty, 5th–6th century.

THE NORTHERN WEI

One of the most successful of the northern dynasties in this period was the Northern Wei (386–534), established by a sinicized Turkic tribe, the Tabgatch or Toba. The Northern Wei ruled a wide area of northern China and for half a century their capital at Pingcheng (present-day Datong in Shanxi province) was the focus of regional power and wealth. Northern Wei tombs have revealed the wide contacts and cultural sophistication of these so-called "barbarian" nomads: discoveries include metalwork bearing Indian, Hellenistic, and Iranian forms and motifs; Roman or Persian glass bowls; and other luxury artifacts.

After flirting with Daoism, the Northern Wei adopted Buddhism as a state religion and under the leadership of the influential monk Tan Yao the new faith spread rapidly. The Northern Wei has left two magnificent Buddhist cave complexes, at Yungang near Datong (construction of which began ca. 460) and at Longmen near Luoyang, begun after the Wei had moved their capital south to the latter city in 494. For a time Longmen was the most important Buddhist center in China, and possibly in the whole of Asia. The outstanding remaining features of these sites are their fine sculptures of Buddhist figures and motifs (see pages 54–55, 66).

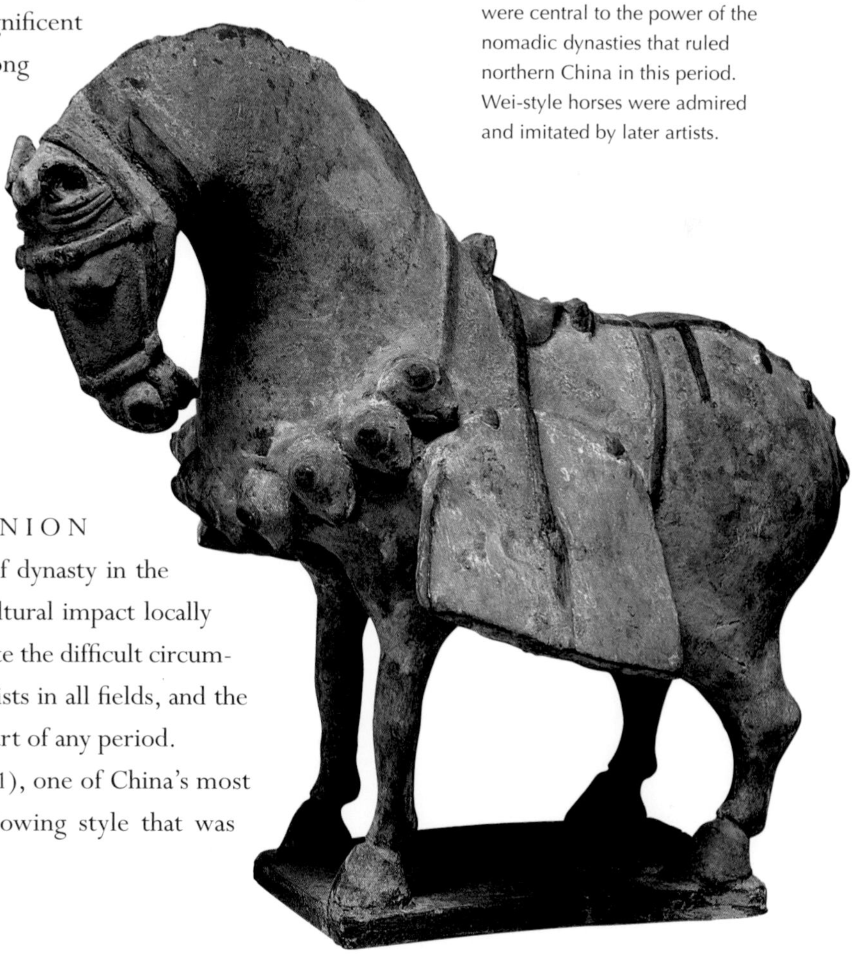

BELOW
A painted terracotta horse dating from the Western Wei dynasty (534–557), one of the successor states to the Northern Wei. Horses were central to the power of the nomadic dynasties that ruled northern China in this period. Wei-style horses were admired and imitated by later artists.

ART IN THE PERIOD OF DISUNION

Wars, economic crises, and frequent changes of dynasty in the Period of Disunion doubtless had a negative cultural impact locally and even nationally from time to time, yet despite the difficult circumstances every dynasty produced outstanding artists in all fields, and the arrival of Buddhism inspired some of the finest art of any period.

The Jin-dynasty artist Wang Xizhi (303–361), one of China's most famous calligraphers, developed a dynamic flowing style that was

an advance on the more rigid Han-dynasty tradition. Wang once entertained forty friends at his rural retreat, the Orchid Pavilion near modern Shaoxing, where each recited his own poetry. Their contributions were gathered in an anthology to which Wang wrote a famous introduction, *The Preface to the Orchid Pavilion Collection*, regarded as one of the greatest calligraphic masterworks (see pages 112–113).

Another famous Jin figure was the painter Gu Kaizhi (344–405). Although his works survive only in copies, his reputation as an artist and a writer on art persisted in later centuries, and he was praised by the eminent ninth-century art historian Zhang Yanyuan. Gu painted landscapes, a tradition already well established in China, and was particularly famed for portraits that not only reproduced a likeness but also conveyed character by facial expression and gesture. This is demonstrated by his two most famous long scrolls: *The Admonitions of the Instructress to the Court Ladies* and *The Goddess of the Luo River*. The *Admonitions*, which survives in a Tang copy (see page 11), illustrates a political parody by Zhuang Hua (ca. 232–300), mocking the excesses of an empress. The work's linear style is found in other paintings of the time as well as in contemporary tombs. Three later copies exist of Gu's illustrations to the *Goddess*, a long part-prose and part-poetic work by Cao Zhi (192–232), a son of the Three Kingdoms ruler Cao Cao.

During this period ceramic production continued, particularly in eastern China, and some outstanding celadon pieces (see page 140) were produced at the Yue kilns in present-day Zhejiang province. The Han tradition of producing pottery *mingqi*, or "spirit objects," persisted throughout this time. These were miniature representations of things felt necessary for the afterlife, such as servants, buildings, horses, and everyday items, as well as hybrid guardian creatures.

LEFT
A painted terracotta figurine of a lady in elegant, pleated robes carrying offerings. This may be a continuation of the Han tradition of producing pottery *mingqi*, or "spirit objects"—small representations of things felt necessary for the afterlife, such as servants. Western Wei dynasty, 535–557 CE.

RIGHT
The Northern Wei dynasty was the first in China to make Buddhism the official state religion. Set against a flaming mandorla (almond-shaped halo), this figure of a *bodhisattva*, an enlightened deity, holds a tall lotus as a symbol of enlightenment. Gilded bronze, Northern Wei dynasty, dated 521 CE.

THE COMING OF THE DHARMA

The Flowering of Buddhism in China

BELOW
The Wanfo (10,000-Buddha) cave at Longmen is named for the thousands of small Buddhas carved on its walls. Shown here is Amitabha flanked by the Buddha's disciples Ananda and Kasyapa and two *bodhisattvas*. Tang dynasty, completed 680 CE.

The Chinese had heard about the Indian religion of the Buddha since the Han expansion into Central Asia under Wu Di (141–87 BCE). According to a traditional story, Ming Di (ruled 58–76), the second emperor of the Eastern Han, dreamed he saw a golden figure with a shining halo who, after appearing in the palace, flew off in a westerly direction. His advisors told him that this must have been the Buddha, who dwelt in India. The emperor thereupon sent two envoys to India to bring back information about the Buddha and his teachings (the Dharma). Three years later, in 67 CE, they returned to the capital, Luoyang, with two senior Buddhist monks, bearing images of the Buddha as well as the *Sutra in Forty-Two Chapters*. The emperor ordered the construction of a Buddhist temple near Luoyang, which was named the White Horse monastery after the animal that bore their precious gifts to China. Over the centuries hundreds more Buddhist monasteries were established in China.

After learning the Chinese language the Indian monks translated the *sutra* (scriptural text) with Chinese collaborators. This was the first of many translations of Buddhist texts during the following centuries, the products of collaboration between Chinese and Indian and Central Asian monks.

It was a little later that the first Buddhist missionaries entered China and started proselytizing. By then Buddhism had been developing for six centuries and had already divided into a number of schools, not all of which advocated retreating from the world to live a life of pious seclusion. Mahayana Buddhism in particular sought to reach out to the mass of ordinary mortals. In addition to the Buddha, Mahayana placed particular stress on the figure of the *bodhisattva*, who had attained enlightenment and thereafter devoted himself or herself to relieving the suffering of humanity and assisting them on their own spiritual progress. *Bodhisattvas* became the subject of widespread popular devotion, along with a

host of other figures such as Maitreya, the Buddha of the future, and other "Celestial Buddhas," as well as Buddhist saints. With its promise of salvation and multiplicity of divinity-like figures, it was the Mahayana form of Buddhism that was to have the most widespread appeal among the Chinese population.

ABOVE
Stupas herald the site of the Mogao caves, near the oasis town of Dunhuang in Gansu, western China. From the 3rd century, Mogao, on the Silk Road, was a key center of Buddhist culture, reaching its high point under the Tang but remaining important until the 14th century. The cave shrines were rediscovered in the early 20th century and yielded hundreds of sculptures, paintings, and texts.

BUDDHISM IN THE PERIOD OF DISUNION

It was at the time of the Jin and the Northern and Southern Dynasties, during the Period of Disunion, that Buddhism made its greatest advances in China. This was partly because they were troubled times when the Mahayana promise of salvation had great appeal to the suffering masses, but also owing to the great mixing of ethnic groups, some of which had already become Buddhists, that occurred in China during this period. Some Northern Dynasties rulers founded Buddhist temples, notably the Northern Wei (see page 63), who sponsored the famous rock-cut temples at Yungang near Datong and Longmen near Luoyang with their magnificent sculptures. In

ABOVE
A representation of the Pure Land, the paradise of the Buddha Amitabha (Amituo Fo), who is depicted on a lotus throne at the top of the scene. *Thangka* (painted banner) on silk, early 10th century. The Pure Land school was dominant at this time.

OPPOSITE
This painted limestone figure of the Buddha was among a cache found in 1996 at the site of a vanished temple in Qingzhou, Shandong province. It is in the sensual, rounded style of the Northern Qi dynasty (550–577).

the Southern Dynasties, one particularly devoted Buddhist ruler, Emperor Wu of Liang (ruled 502–549), left his throne for long periods to pass his time in study and meditation in a monastery. He imitated the asceticism of the Buddha, ate only one meal a day, and abstained not only from meat but also from garlic and onions, which might arouse the passions. He also forbade the slaughter of actual animals in sacrifices, instead having representations of the animals made out of flour.

By then many Buddhist *sutras* had been translated into Chinese by, among others, Kumarajiva (344–413), a Central Asian who had spent much time in India. Kumarajiva oversaw a translation bureau based in the northern capital of Chang'an (modern Xi'an) that rendered a great range of Indian Buddhist texts from Sanskrit into Chinese, notably the works of the second-century scholar Nagarjuna and writings of the *Perfection of Wisdom* (*Prajñaparamita*) tradition that were central to the Mahayana school. The *Lotus Sutra* and the *Diamond Sutra* were among the most widely read and chanted texts; a printed copy of Kumarajiva's Chinese translation of the *Diamond Sutra* was discovered in 1907 in the Buddhist caves at Mogao near the Silk Road oasis of Dunhuang and bears the date 868 CE, making it the world's oldest printed book.

PATHS OF WISDOM: PURE LAND AND CHAN

The two schools of Buddhism that became most widespread in China were Pure Land and Chan (Japanese: Zen). The former was based on the Mahayana cult of Amitabha (Amituo Fo in Chinese), the Buddha of Infinite Radiance, promising that those who called on his name would be reborn in a celestial paradise called the Pure Land, where they could live blissfully without having attained enlightenment on Earth. When the cult arrived in China, it was necessary merely to recite the mantra *Nianfo Amituo Fo* (Homage to Amitabha Buddha) to attain the Pure Land. Promoted by Hui Yan (334–416), a learned monk who was posthumously named the first patriarch of Pure Land, the cult became particularly popular in the south. In Mahayana cosmology, Amitabha

ABOVE
Maitreya (Mile Fo), the messiah-like Buddha of the future age, was the focus of various popular movements in Chinese history. This colossal stone representation—at 234 ft. (71 m) the world's largest stone Buddha—was carved between 713 and 803 in the cliffs at Leshan, Sichuan province (see also pages 54–55).

was manifest on earth in the form of Avalokiteshvara, the *bodhisattva* of compassion. In China under the Sui and especially the Tang, images of this male deity, the embodiment of loving-kindness, became increasingly sensual and feminized, and Avalokiteshvara was ultimately transformed into Guanyin, the "goddess of mercy," who has always been one of the most popular Chinese deities. She is frequently portrayed bearing Amitabha, her spiritual progenitor, in her headgear.

Chan, the school of meditation (Sanskrit *dhyana*, whence Chinese *chan*), is said to have been brought to China by the Indian monk Bodhidharma in the early sixth century. According to this school, enlightenment came not through the intellectual study of written texts or by performing elaborate rituals, but by arriving at insight and wisdom through quiet introspection and meditation. Chan masters preferred to teach orally, and their dialogues and *gong an* (paradoxical conundrums, whence the Japanese *koan*) were highly influential when Chan was subsequently transmitted to Korea and Japan as Son and Zen respectively. The Chan ideals of introspection and simplicity

influenced Chinese painters, whose working method often involved a period of contemplation in order to comprehend the essence of the subject, followed by rapid execution with free brushwork.

ZENITH UNDER THE TANG

In the Sui and Tang dynasties Buddhism continued to flourish in a reunited China. During the first two centuries of Tang rule, it from time to time benefited from imperial patronage, for example under Taizong (ruled 626–649) and the empress Wu Zetian (ruled 690–705). The work of translating Buddhist texts into Chinese continued all the while. In 629 the Buddhist scholar Xuanzang (602–664) set out on an epic journey to India, returning in 647 to Chang'an (modern Xi'an) with a great treasury of Buddhist scriptures, precious images, and relics, and was welcomed with great acclaim by the emperor Taizong. Xuanzang spent the rest of his life directing teams of translators, who between them translated a quarter of all the Chinese versions of Indian Buddhist texts.

ABOVE AND OPPOSITE, RIGHT
Built from 460 in a sandstone cliff-face near the Northern Wei capital of Pingcheng (modern Datong), the site at Yungang has over 50 caves containing more than 50,000 carved and painted Buddhist figures. As shown in Cave no.12 (opposite, right, and above, with Maitreya Buddha), with its colorful dancing figures, the Buddhist art of the Northern Wei dynasty represents a transition from Indian and Central Asian styles toward purely Chinese ones. Cave no.12, dated 483, is particularly noted for its depictions of ancient Chinese musical instruments.

RIGHT

A pagoda is the distinctly Chinese form of the Buddhist stupa, or reliquary monument. Stupas were built to house relics of the Buddha (such as a bone or tooth), as memorials to holy figures, or as repositories for sacred scriptures and images. The latter was the original function of the Great Wild Goose Pagoda in Xi'an, which was built in 652 to house the hundreds of Buddhist scriptures brought to China from India by the scholar Xuanzang. Early pagodas were originally square in plan, but after the Tang dynasty 10- and even 12-sided structures became more common.

Still standing today, the Great Wild Goose Pagoda in Xi'an was built as a home for the many writings that Xuanzang accumulated on his travels.

The only woman ever to style herself "emperor," Wu Zetian (690–705) was also a fervent Buddhist. Her devotion is most spectacularly seen at the Longmen caves near Luoyang, which had been founded by the Northern Wei dynasty in the 490s. Among her commissions there is Longmen's largest cave temple, the Fengxian, for which a space 115 ft. (35 m) wide and 128 ft. (39 m) high was hewn from solid rock. The temple contains a colossal 56 ft (17 m) statue of Vairochana, one of the Celestial Buddhas, whose facial features were reputedly modeled on those of the empress herself. This and other images at Longmen show how Chinese Buddhist art had acquired an entirely native style that was very different from its Indian and Central Asian models.

A FALL FROM GRACE

During the ninth century, as the power of the Tang emperors declined, an anti-Buddhist movement arose first among Daoists and then Confucian officials and scholars. On the one hand, Buddhism was seen as a foreign religion; on the other hand there was resentment at the immense wealth and land that monasteries had acquired. The anti-Buddhist movement started in the field of literary style with a conservative movement that advocated a return to the classical style of writing and a rejection of the experimentation with new literary themes and forms fashionable during the Southern Dynasties. In 819 the great prose writer Han Yu (768–824), who is viewed as a pioneer of the Confucian revival, wrote a famous diatribe about the mass hysteria accompanying the moving of a Buddhist relic.

The next stage came in 845 with the proscription of all foreign religions including, and especially, Buddhism, which was accused of undermining public morality. There were also political reasons for the ban. One was the power of the court eunuchs, many of whom were devoted Buddhists. Another was the Buddhists' accumulation of wealth, including their great use of bronze and other metals for bells, statues, and other devotional artifacts, at a time when the state was running short of coins. Many monasteries were closed and either demolished or converted to other use. A limited number were allowed to continue, with a much reduced number of monks.

Buddhism continued in China, and at times even flourished—for example under the foreign Yuan and Qing dynasties, whose rulers were themselves Buddhists—but it would never again attain the immense prestige and status it had enjoyed during its zenith in the Period of Disunion and the early Tang.

DAZU

Caves of the Buddha

Situated fifteen miles (24 km) from Chongqing in eastern Sichuan province, the Buddhist cave shrines of Dazu ("Big Foot"), rediscovered only in 1945, take their name from a legend that the Buddha himself left a giant footprint here. In fact, work on the caves began in 650 at the behest of the local Tang governor and continued through the Tang and Song dynasties. Local officials, gentry, monks, nuns, and other individuals lent support, and small statues of some of the donors stand beside those of giant Buddhas. With their marvellous quality, excellent state of preservation, and wide range of imagery, the Dazu sculptures are as impressive as the better known cave shrines of the north.

Dazu is in fact not one site but many—there are more than seventy individual sites containing altogether some 50,000 statues, carved into the faces of the cliffs. The two

BELOW
The shrine of Mahapoya, the Buddha of Great Appropriate Means, carved into the cliff-face at Baodingshan, Dazu. The shrine tells the story of the Buddha's acts of filial piety or devotion in both his final existence and his previous lives. At the center is the figure of the Buddha himself, which stands some 11.5 ft. (3.5 m) high. Song dynasty.

LEFT

"The Grotto of the Revolving Wheel" at Baodingshan, Dazu. Six feet (2 m) in diameter, it depicts the six realms of existence into which the soul can be reborn, with hell at the bottom and the Western Paradise of Amitabha at the top. The other realms are those of the gods, humans, animals, and hungry ghosts. At the base are figures representing the human failings that ensure that the cycle of rebirth continues: greed, hatred, and delusion. The whole wheel is gripped by Yama, the god of death, from whom one may escape only by attaining an enlightenment-induced transcendental state of release, or *nirvana*. The figure at the center of the wheel is thought by some to be a portrait of Zhao Zhifeng, the shrine's founder.

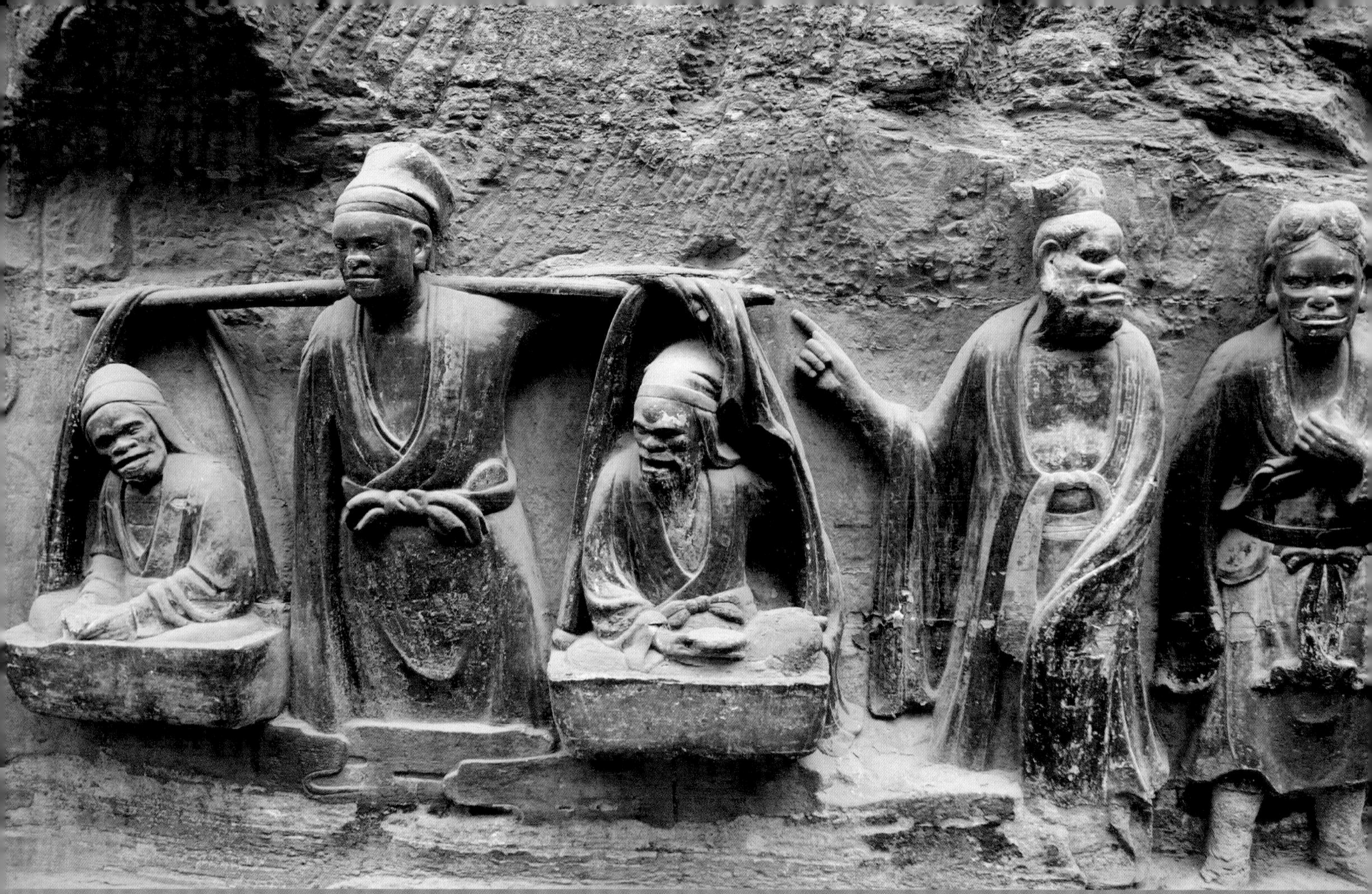

ABOVE
The Dazu grottoes are remarkable for their vivid, naturalistic portrayals of ordinary people. The carvings also blend Buddhist concepts with Daoist and Confucian ones, as in this detail from the scene shown on page 74, showing a beggar carrying his aged parents, illustrating the Confucian ideal of filial piety.

main clusters of shrines are at Beishan (North Hill) and Baodingshan (Precious Peak Hill), the latter largely the responsibility of a key figure in the development of Dazu, the monk Zhao Zhifeng (born ca. 1159), who is said to have devoted seventy years to directing the expansion of the grottoes. The Tang figures at Dazu are generally plump and well built, reflecting the contemporary fashion; the Song figures in contrast are more slender and elegant.

THE GROTTO OF THE REVOLVING WHEEL

Baodingshan is the biggest single site at Dazu with more than 10,000 statues. It was near here that Shakyamuni supposedly left his gigantic footprint and it was here too that Zhao Zhifeng spent most of his time supervising the sculptors: the complex includes a shrine to his memory. Zhao Zhifeng belonged to an esoteric Tantric sect of Buddhism, which in the north of China did not survive the persecutions of the late Tang, but flourished in the south for a few more centuries. Baodingshan was one of its main centers.

The largest and most famous shrine here is number three, which dates to the Song dynasty and is known as "The Grotto of the Revolving Wheel" (see illustration page 75). Depicting the Wheel of Life, it stands parallel to the ground on eight pillars at the entrance to the grotto. The wheel symbolizes *samsara*, the cycle of existence that is

broken only by following the Buddha's teaching, known as the Dharma (represented in Buddhist iconography by a wheel), to obtain *nirvana* and release from endless rebirths and the suffering that they entail. Inside the grotto—and symbolically outside the wheel of existence, from which he has escaped—is the main figure of the Buddha on his lotus throne, flanked by disciples, *bodhisattva*s, children, and donors. The entrance is flanked by fierce guardians to ward off evil spirits.

Another special feature of Baodingshan is a series of sculpted tableaux depicting the Buddhist hell, which includes drunkards, lechers, and murderers. Amid these sometimes horrific scenes the figure of a *bodhisattva* offers salvation. One of the most remarkable features of Baodingshan, and of Dazu as a whole, are its lively and sympathetic depictions of ordinary people and rural life. Figures include a beggar devotedly carrying his aged and emaciated parents, and the very expressive face of a disciple watching the scene with mixed emotions. Some of the sculptures of Buddhist deities, such as Guanyin, are also rendered in a natural and lifelike way.

Another unusual feature of Dazu is that, while overwhelmingly Buddhist, the site also includes Confucian and Daoist figures, perhaps because Dazu was looked on as the major religious center for the region as a whole. The donors at Baodingshan, for example, included Wei Lioaweng, a famous Confucian scholar of the Song dynasty.

ABOVE
A detail of a sculpture of the Buddha's death, or Final Nirvana, at Baodingshan, showing the head of the recumbent Buddha and a group of his disciples and donors, including the curly-haired figure of Zhao Zhifeng, the shrine's creator. Song dynasty.

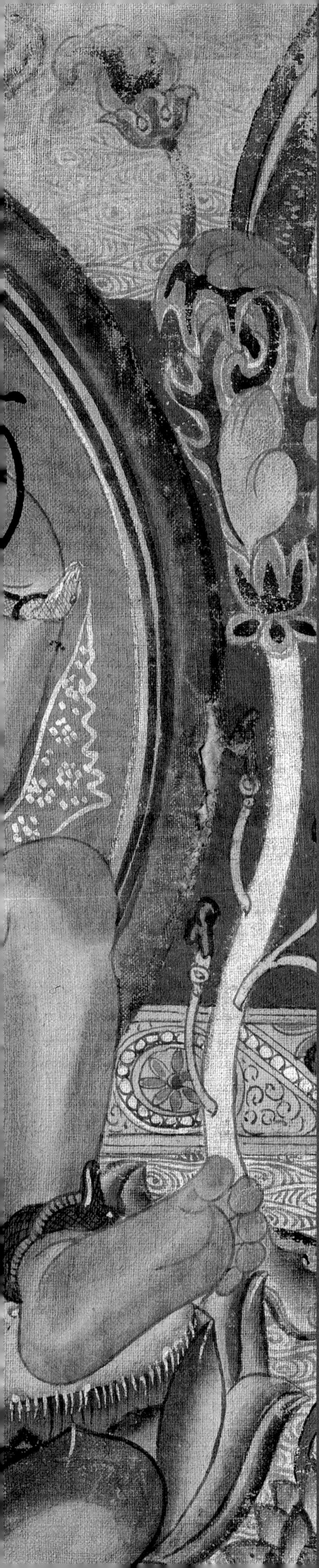

四

CHAPTER FOUR

A GOLDEN AGE

581– 907 CE

THE ERA OF THE TANG

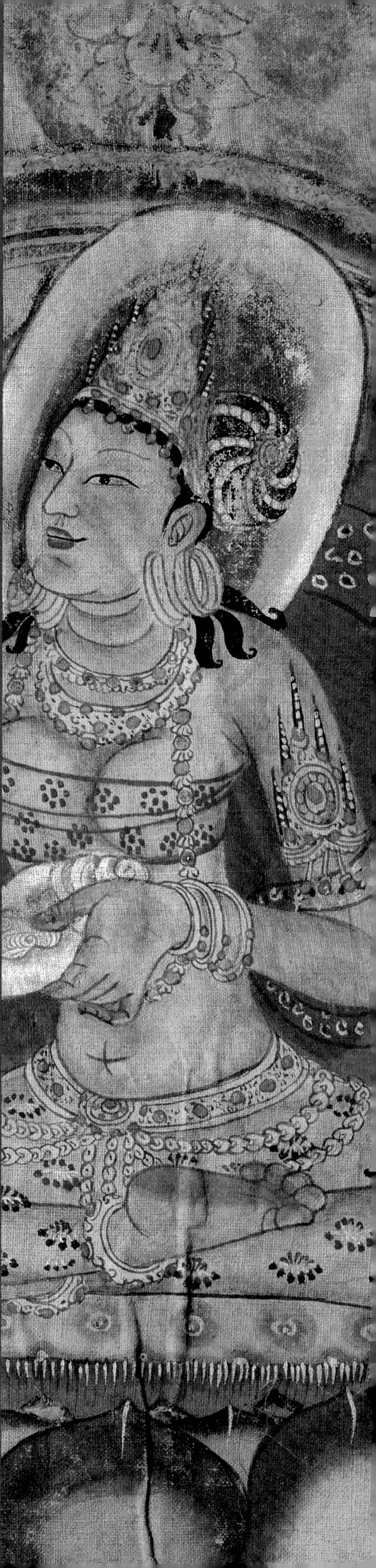

隋

A REUNITED EMPIRE

The Sui Dynasty (581–618)

隋 In 581 Yang Jian, an aristocratic general of the shortlived Northern Zhou dynasty, staged a coup d'etat and set up a new dynasty in the north, the Sui. Yang Jian reigned until 604 with the imperial title Wen Di. Within eight years he had conquered the last remaining southern dynasty, the Chen (557–589), and reunified China after three and a half centuries of division.

Although the Sui dynasty itself proved to be shortlived, it left an enduring mark on imperial China, much as the Qin had done eight hundred years earlier. Wen Di set up a united central administration including six ministries (public administration, finance, rites, war, justice, and public works), and restored the system of prefectures and counties first introduced by the Qin, though over a much larger area than the Qin had ruled. He initiated an examination for civil servants that was much more comprehensive than similar experiments by the Han dynasty, and decreed that the appointment and dismissal of officials was the prerogative of the central government. Wen Di also took measures to boost the economy by lightening the tax burden on the population.

CONNECTING THE EMPIRE: THE GRAND CANAL

Perhaps the most memorable achievement of Wen Di and his son and successor, Yang Di (604–618), was the completion of a new "Grand Canal" to link northern and southern China. Except for the sea, there is no natural transportation route connecting the north of China, where the imperial capitals were usually located, with the south. But by the sixth century imperial governments had come to depend on the transportation of grain

LEFT
The two Sui emperors were devout Buddhists and commissioned many Buddhist images, including this one of Amitabha Buddha (Amituo Fo) from Chongguang temple in Hancui village, Hebei. The solid form and flat folds of drapery are typical of the Sui. Marble, reign of Wen Di, with an inscription dated 585.

RIGHT
The Grand Canal ranks with the Great Wall as a feat of construction. In this 18th-century painting the emperor Yang Di, second ruler of the Sui dynasty, is depicted on the imperial bark (lower right) inspecting the works to extend the canal to Hangzhou. Painting on silk, Qing dynasty, reign of Qianlong (1736–1795).

ABOVE
A caravan of merchants on the Silk Road is depicted in this Sui-dynasty wall painting from the Buddhist shrines at Mogao near Dunhuang in western China. Dunhuang was an important oasis on the road linking China with India and Central Asia and from the 4th to the 14th centuries was home to a rich and cosmopolitan Buddhist culture, which enjoyed its zenith in the Sui–Tang era.

from the south to feed both the capital and Chinese armies on the northern frontiers. The Han had already constructed canals to link Chang'an—which, being so far inland, was particularly difficult to supply—to the North China Plain. The Grand Canal, as conceived by Wen Di and implemented by his successor, involved rebuilding existing canals and digging new channels to link the Yangzi and Yellow rivers, and continuing south of the Yangzi across the eastern plains as far as Hangzhou in Zhejiang province.

The result was the world's longest artificial waterway. Although contemporary writers condemned Yang Di for the great burden of labor service that he demanded in order to complete the Grand Canal, it did succeed in strengthening the newly reunified state both economically and militarily. The canal—still in use today—made the comparative wealth of the south available to the north, and was particularly important for conveying southern taxation rice to the government in the capital Chang'an.

Yang Di rebuilt both Chang'an and the other northern capital, Luoyang, on a grand scale, laying both out on a grid with the main avenues running north–south and east–west. In conjunction with these projects he built two large granaries near the two capitals to ensure a steady supply of grain for the two major centers of population.

The emperor also built a third imperial capital, Yang Du (Yangzhou), where the Grand Canal meets the Yangzi River. Here the Sui built a navy and launched expeditions to Taiwan, Sumatra, and what is now Vietnam These projects had also been initiated by Wen Di, but were brought to fruition by his son.

Because of his supposed extravagance and love of luxury, Yang Di has been condemned by historians for causing the downfall of the Sui dynasty. But it was more probably the cost of repeated military expeditions against the Koreans in the east, who had allied themselves with Turkic peoples in the west, that undermined the economy. Whatever the cause, there was a rebellion against the dynasty in 613 and it was eventually overthrown by one of its own generals in 618.

ACHIEVEMENTS AND ARTISTRY OF THE SUI

After the Grand Canal, no single monument illustrates the new spirit of confidence that permeated all strata of society under the Sui better than the arched bridge across the Jiao River at Zhaozhou in Hebei province, China's oldest surviving stone bridge. At each end of its shallow arch—its single span is longer than that of any bridge built in Europe before the Renaissance—are two open spandrels designed to reduce the force of floodwaters and save the structure of the bridge from damage. In addition, its balustrades are decorated with superb relief carvings of animals and vegetation.

Work continued on the major Buddhist grottoes, the quality of murals making notable advances. One particularly dramatic painting in cave no. 397 at Dunhuang entitled *Crossing the City Wall at Midnight* shows the young Shakyamuni (Buddha), determined to leave home in order to seek enlightenment, being helped to fly over the city gate on his horse by a god, while his parents try to persuade him not to go. He is accompanied by angel-like spirits playing music and defended by spirit guards as the god raises his horse's hoofs upwards and he rides off into the mountains. This and many other Sui-dynasty murals are full of movement and energy and are both dramatic and colorful.

Secular painting also flourished. One artist, Zhan Ziqian, who was an official of the Sui government, inspired Tang-dynasty painters to the extent that he was called "the Ancestor of Tang Painting." One of his landscapes, *Taking a Walk in Spring*, displays several features that came to be adopted by Tang and Song artists, such as human figures shown as minute compared to the grandeur of nature, and space organized so that trees and mountains each appeared in their proper relation to each other. Zhan Ziqian was also adept at depicting human expression in his figurative painting, palace buildings and gardens in his landscapes, and incidents from historical stories.

唐

THE GREAT PROGENITOR

Taizong and the Early Tang, 618–705

BELOW
A pendant decorated in relief on both sides and set in a gilded bronze beaded frame. The side shown here depicts a monkey playing among grapevines; the motif of vines is probably of Iranian origin, reflecting the cosmopolitan influences on Tang art. Calcified white jade, early Tang, 7th century.

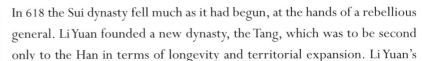

唐 In 618 the Sui dynasty fell much as it had begun, at the hands of a rebellious general. Li Yuan founded a new dynasty, the Tang, which was to be second only to the Han in terms of longevity and territorial expansion. Li Yuan's own reign ended inauspiciously in 626, when a family quarrel resulted in his own death and that of his two elder sons. The throne fell to his third son, Li Shimin, who as a very young man had proven his leadership qualities by winning battles on behalf of his father. Ruling (626–649) under the title Tang Taizong (Great Progenitor of the Tang), he was destined to become one of the most successful emperors in Chinese history.

As soon as he had consolidated his power, Taizong set to work on reforming the administrative system established by the Sui. At the heart of the Tang system of government were four main departments: the Department of State Affairs, including the six ministries (see page 80); the Imperial Chancellery, which checked and transmitted imperial decrees; the Grand Secretariat, responsible for drafting official texts; and the State Council, including the emperor and the most important civil servants. There were other central offices, such as the Court of Censors, or Inspectorate, which heard complaints from the public and oversaw the conduct of civil servants, and the High Court of Justice, which gave decisions on the most complex legal cases and alone had the right to pronounce the death penalty. These offices between them supervised the various tiers of bureaucracy throughout the empire at the level of counties, prefectures, and special administrative regions. Other offices controlled canals and waterways, arsenals, and so on. This administrative structure was retained, with minor changes, by the major dynasties of China.

A COSMOPOLITAN CAPITAL: CHANG'AN

The Tang inherited their capital, Chang'an (modern Xi'an), from the Sui. It was built on a square plan, about six miles (10 km) from east to west and five miles (8 km) from north to south, with fourteen broad avenues running north to south and eleven running east to west. Between these avenues were 110 walled areas and two large markets, one in the east and one in the west. In the north of the city were

two large walled areas containing the Imperial City, and, immediately south of it, the Administrative City. Most of the main capital cities of subsequent dynasties, including the last two, the Ming and Qing, followed the Sui–Tang plan, as did some other towns in China. The plan followed the Chinese cosmological notion that the sky was round and the Earth—of which Chang'an was a symbolic microcosm—was square, and that to be successful a ruler should sit on his throne and face south, as the mythical emperor Shun (see pages 16–17) was said to have done.

Surrounding Chang'an city were imperial parks and other palace buildings, while canals joined with river systems flowing from a mountain range beyond the plain in the south to lead fresh water directly into the markets.

In the early Middle Ages, Chang'an was the biggest city in the world with a million inhabitants and a population that included thousands of foreign merchants, students, and entertainers. Among the city's visitors were merchants from as far west as Samarkand and Bukhara, and foreign diplomats from even farther afield. An embassy from

ABOVE
Banquet and Concert, an anonymous painting depicting ladies of the Tang court enjoying a feast with musical accompaniment. Such musical instruments might have their wooden surfaces decorated with lacquerwork. For millennia music had been an important element of Chinese court life because it was believed to connect descendants with the spirits of their forefathers. Late Tang or early Five Dynasties period, 10th century.

ABOVE
Iranian influence is displayed in this gold bowl from near Chang'an, the ancient capital of the Tang, with incised motifs of deer, birds, and flowers. However, the lotus petal pattern is Buddhist in origin. Tang dynasty, mid-8th century.

OPPOSITE
This warrior's sophisticated armor is held in place by a complex system of straps and cords. The exact origin of the figure, 2 ft. 4 in. (72 cm) high, is unknown, but a pair made from identical molds and dated 664 was discovered guarding the sloping ramp leading to the tomb chamber of a commander of Emperor Taizong's bodyguard. Glazed earthenware, Tang dynasty, ca. 664.

Sasanian Iran arrived in Chang'an in 632, and one from the Byzantine empire visited the imperial capital a few years later in 643.

Foreign religious beliefs also made their way east. Nestorianism, a nonorthodox school of Christianity that had been banned in the Byzantine empire in the fifth century, was disseminated along the Silk Road from Iran and arrived at Chang'an in 631. The Tang court authorized the Nestorians to preach and this form of Christianity—known in China as Jingjiao or the Luminous Religion—thrived for a time. An important Nestorian text, in Chinese, has been preserved on a stone tablet from Chang'an.

Other foreign religions that penetrated China in this period included Manicheism, which became an authorized cult at the end of the seventh century and had some influence on Chinese astronomy, and Zoroastrianism, which had been expelled from Iran following Arab invasions and the arrival of Islam.

Zoroastrian beliefs and rites made no lasting impact on Chinese culture, but Chinese craftsmen did learn practical skills through their contacts with Iranians, including techniques of hammering and chiseling gold and silver, while the Chinese elite took up the game of polo, which was of Iranian origin.

The Tang state also sponsored Daoism, as well as Buddhism, the most successful "foreign" religion in China. While the numbers of temples, monks, and priests were restricted, religious institutions were exempt from taxation and Buddhist monasteries

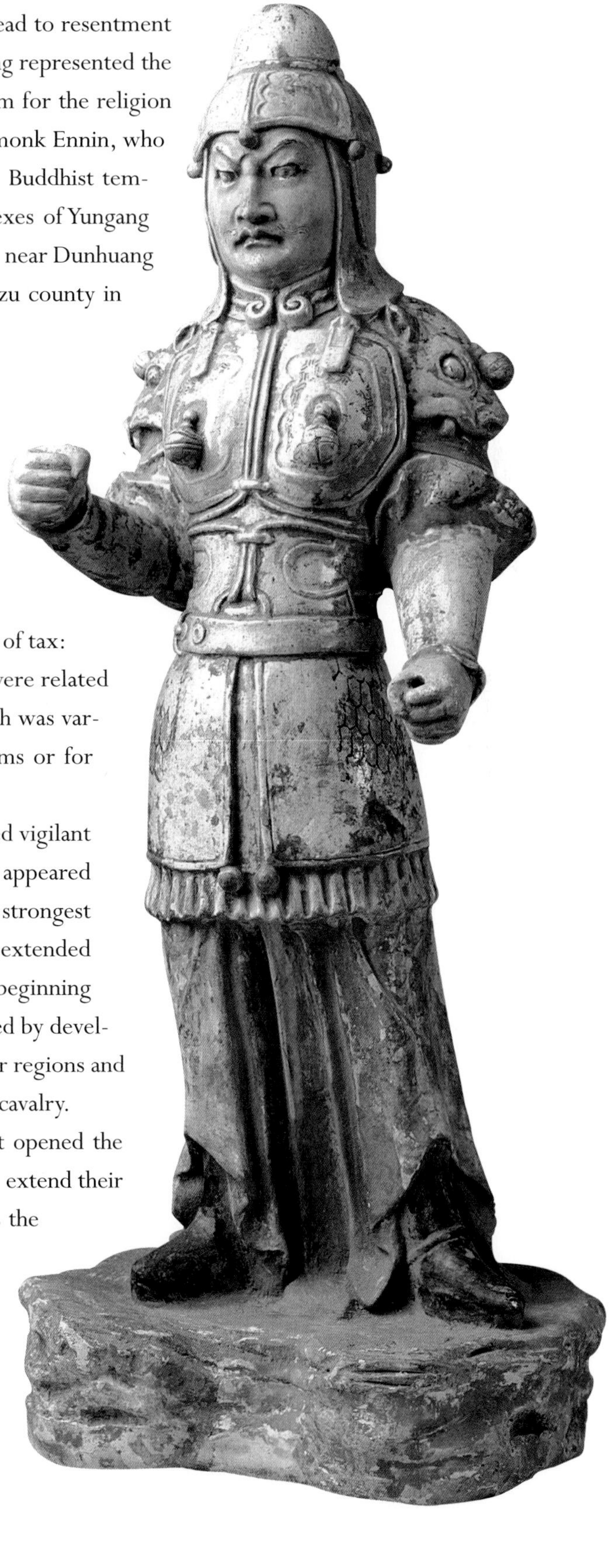

accumulated large estates, a fact which, later in the dynasty, would lead to resentment that fueled a growing anti-Buddhist movement (see page 73). The Tang represented the zenith of Buddhism in China, and the widespread popular enthusiasm for the religion in this period had a profound effect on Japanese visitors such as the monk Ennin, who in 838 visited the sacred Mount Wutai, where alone more than 300 Buddhist temples were constructed during the dynasty. The cave-temple complexes of Yungang and Longmen were expanded under the Tang, as were those of Mogao near Dunhuang in the far west of the empire. In the south, the first grottoes of Dazu county in Sichuan date from this period (see pages 74–77).

PROSPERITY AND EXPANSION

Tang economic prosperity was based on new and imaginative agrarian regulations called the "equal distribution of land." According to these regulations every family was granted enough land to support itself. The system also facilitated the payment of taxes, which were levied on people rather than land, and depended on the number of adult males in the family. There were several kinds of tax: a tax on grain, corvee (labor service), and a tax on cloth. All taxes were related to the conditions that prevailed locally; for example, the tax on cloth was varied according to whether an area was suitable for rearing silkworms or for producing plant fiber.

Notwithstanding its internal prosperity, the Tang empire remained vigilant against external threats. During the sixth century a new menace had appeared on the northern frontiers in the form of Turks, who had defeated the strongest of the other peoples in the region. To defend their empire the Sui had extended the Great Wall westward nearly to its present western end. At the beginning of the Tang the Turks still presented a threat, which the Tang countered by developing its military power, recruiting skilled horsemen from the border regions and organizing stud farms to ensure a supply of superior horses for their cavalry.

In 630 Taizong launched a major offensive against the Turks that opened the way to Central Asia. In the next fifteen years the Chinese were able to extend their administration to Samarkand, Bukhara, and Tashkent. Soon after this the Tang turned their attention northeast to Manchuria and to Korea, where they controlled most of the peninsula, and southeast to Hanoi in present-day Vietnam. To govern these territories the dynasty

十八年五帝共
滅佛法
帝楊堅在位廿

created six military protectorates. Before the end of the seventh century, the Tibetans in Central Asia and the Arabs based in Iran had begun to erode these relatively new areas of influence, but it was not until the middle of the eighth century that troubles in Chang'an led to a serious challenge to Chinese power in Central and East Asia (see pages 94–97).

A WOMAN IN POWER: EMPRESS WU

After the death in 683 of Taizong's successor, Gaozong, power fell into the hands of a figure unique in Chinese history, the female emperor Wu Zetian. Women often wielded considerable power at court, especially if a filial emperor had a feisty mother, and there had been other cases when they had assumed supreme power. But Wu, a concubine of both Taizong and Gaozong who had climbed her way up by court intrigue, was unique in assuming the title "emperor." Effective ruler during the reign of Ruizong (684–690), in 690 Wu proclaimed a new dynasty, the Zhou, which interrupted the Tang for fifteen years.

The empress's main enemies were the traditional aristocracy of the Chang'an region. She put many of them to death and to ensure that their families would not retaliate at court she promoted the state examination system as the only means of recruiting imperial officials. From a historical point of view this was a positive step. From then on until almost the end of the Qing dynasty period, the examination system continued to play a major part in Chinese government and education, ensuring that China's bureaucrats were chosen, for the most part, on the basis of merit rather than patronage.

Wu was a devout and enthusiastic Buddhist and received support from the court eunuchs, many of whom were also Buddhists. It was even asserted among some of her followers that she was an incarnation of Maitreya, the Buddha of the future. She liked to get away from Chang'an and spent much of her reign in the eastern capital, Luoyang, donating large sums and many treasures to Buddhist institutions.

OPPOSITE
Emperor Wu Di of Han (ruled 141–87 BCE), from a celebrated series of portraits of past emperors by the Tang master Yan Liben (ca. 600–673). He subtly yet powerfully conveys the character of the ruler with restrained color and a tightly disciplined line. Ink and pigment on silk, ca. 650–670.

BELOW
Attitudes toward the role of women were more liberal under the Tang than most other dynasties, as indicated by this lively painted earthenware figure of a woman playing polo, a sport imported from Iran that was popular with the Tang elite of both sexes. Tang, 7th–8th century.

TANG IMPERIAL TOMBS

Cities for the Afterlife

When Tang Taizong died in 649, the site he selected for his tomb in Liquan county, Shaanxi province, some thirty-six miles (60 km) from Chang'an, was dug into the south face of a natural rocky hill, Mount Jiuzong, the peak of which served as a grave mound. The choice of such an impressive place for his tomb shows that Taizong was well aware of the importance of his place in history. It also established the Tang rulers' custom of using natural hills as the sites of their tombs. In spite of his warnings to his family against extravagance, no expense was spared, and his final resting place was by far the biggest of all the Tang tombs, with a vast coffin chamber and more than thirty burial spaces reserved for his closest relatives.

The tomb of the Empress Wu Zetian is also on a hill, not quite so far from Chang'an, but is better preserved.

ABOVE
Guardian figures of horses and their grooms line the *shen dao* or "spirit path" to the joint tomb of Emperor Gaozong and Empress Wu on Liangshan Hill, 50 miles (80 km) northwest of the Tang capital, Chang'an (Xi'an).

ABOVE
A falconer. Since the 1950s more than 20 tombs in Shaanxi province have yielded magnificent murals that constitute the most important extant body of original Tang painting. Early Tang, 7th century.

RIGHT
A memorial stela at Zhaoling, the tomb of the emperor Taizong, Shaanxi. Some 36 miles (60 km) in circumference, Zhaoling included 167 attendant tombs of nobles, officials, and military commanders.

昭陵
时 代：唐
编号：170
分类号：9
礼泉县人民政府

There was a dispute as to whether it would be right for her to be buried with her former lover, the emperor Gaozong, but it was finally allowed. The joint mausoleum was designed according to tradition on a north to south axis, and is approached by a long straight path from the south, lined with 124 stone sculptures of animals and human figures, including sixty-one foreign emissaries, now unfortunately all decapitated. Nearby stands a memorial stone, which Wu Zetian herself reputedly ordered should remain blank, since it was for posterity, not her, to judge her record.

While smaller in scale, other royal tombs have yielded marvellous finds. One of the most exceptional is that of the tragic Princess Yongtai, who lived during Wu Zetian's reign. Falsely accused of plotting to kill the empress, Yongtai was put to death. She was later entirely exonerated and in a fit of remorse the empress had her interred in a splendid tomb of her own, decorated by murals depicting court ladies waiting on the princess.

ABOVE
Ladies of the court, a mural from the tomb of Princess Yongtai (died 701). The piled hairstyle was a Tang fashion, as were the long sleeves that covered the hands and made manual work impractical—denoting the wearer's aristocratic status. Tang dynasty, reign of Empress Wu Zetian.

RIGHT
A stone lion and a contingent of now headless ambassadors before the tomb mound of Emperor Gaozong and Empress Wu Zetian. The name of the envoy and the country he came from was inscribed on the back of each statue; when and why the figures were mutilated is uncertain.

唐

MASTERS OF EAST ASIA

Tang Zenith and Decline, 705–907

唐 The empress Wu died in 705 and, following the brief reigns of the two predecessors she had ousted, the Tang resumed full control of power under Li Longji, a son of the emperor Ruizong. As the emperor Xuanzong (ruled 712–756), he soon set to work restoring the national finances and those parts of the administration that been disrupted. His reign coincided with the most prosperous period in the Tang dynasty, and it was fitting that Li Longji is also known as Tang Ming Huang (Brilliant Tang Emperor).

Toward the end of his reign Xuanzong gradually lost his grip on state affairs and concentrated on his own personal interests. He patronized the arts and trained a troupe of young musicians and dancers at his palace in his so-called Pear Garden, a name that is still used as a term for the theater. He himself could sing and write poetry, and he invited the famous poet Li Bai to his court. Despite his title, Xuanzong's reign—and with it the heyday of the Tang—ended anything but brilliantly. His extravagant lifestyle was partly to blame for his undoing. He had become besotted with an imperial concubine, Yang Guifei, a relative of Yang Guozhong, a court official who had amassed great wealth and power. To put a check on the Yang family, another official, who was effectively head of the Tang administration, favored the military officials of the northern armies, especially those of foreign descent. He thought that, being outsiders, they would not interfere with court affairs. He was wrong, and this mistake was a major cause of the events that were to follow.

BELOW
Essential for transporting exotic goods along the Silk Road to northern China, camels were a symbol of prosperity in the Tang and models of them are often found in wealthy tombs. The driver of this Bactrian camel wears distinctive Central Asian dress—the Chinese never rode camels themselves. Terracotta, Tang dynasty, second half of the 7th century.

REBELLION AND AFTERMATH

The middle of the eighth century was marked by a rebellion that shook the Tang dynasty to its foundations, and from which it never really recovered. It

was led by Anlushan, one of the northern commanders who had been favored by the head of the administration. Of Turkic descent, Anlushan ("Alexander") controlled three military regions covering most of the modern provinces of Hebei, Shandong, and Shanxi from his base near present-day Beijing, and had at his disposal a quarter of a million men and thirty thousand horses. When his patron at court died, Anlushan feared for his position and in 755 he descended with armies on the capital. Tang resistance rapidly collapsed and the emperor and his concubine Yang Guifei fled with an escort toward Sichuan, Yang Guozhong's home base. On the way the escort refused to continue the journey while Yang Guifei was alive, holding her responsible for the debacle, so she was put to death. This episode was an inspiration to many later poets, playwrights, and painters (see pages 98–99).

Anlushan died in 757 but it was not until 763 that the dynasty regained control, largely with the assistance of Tibetan and Uighur troops. After a painful period of recovery the Tang regained some of its former glory, but the old system of heavily centralized administration had been undermined, with Tibetans and military governors effectively controlling much of the north. The Tang system of land tenure and taxation had gradually broken down under the strain of trying to maintain it in changed conditions. Many landlords and merchants were becoming richer and more powerful, enabling them to acquire large estates and dispossessing many peasants in the process. To make good its fiscal deficits the government began to base its taxation system on actual wealth, reestablished its monopoly on salt and alcohol, and introduced a monopoly on tea. Before long the salt monopoly alone was providing half the government revenue.

ABOVE
A small-stem drinking cup decorated with a relief of a mounted huntsman. Like the gold bowl on page 86, the style of engraving and the decorative detail reflect the influence of Iranian metalworking techniques and motifs. Silver, Tang dynasty.

TANG DECLINE AND FALL

Toward the end of the ninth century the Tang dynasty was shaken once more, this time by widespread peasant revolts. The rebellion led by Huang Chao, a salt smuggler,

RIGHT
A fierce Buddhist tomb guardian or *lokapala* trampling a demon. It is made in the characteristic Tang *sancai* "three-color" low-fired ware with white, green, and amber glaze. Such figures usually stood at the entrances to temples, and smaller versions such as this were popular Tang grave goods. The *lokapala* wears a headdress of a Chinese phoenix (*fenghuang*), an auspicious symbol. Lead-glazed earthenware, Tang dynasty.

attacked county towns killing rich landowners and merchants. He gradually attracted more and more followers until they numbered over half a million. From Shandong they roamed over many provinces, going as far east as Zhejiang and as far south as Guangzhou (Canton), where they massacred rich foreign merchants, including many Arabs—antipathy toward foreigners, as demonstrated in the proscription of Buddhism and other "foreign" religions in 845, had been steadily growing in the later Tang.

Returning north, Huang Chao's followers finally reached Chang'an in 881 and subjected it to a bloodbath. They were expelled from the capital by a Tang general, but the imperial power from then on was merely nominal. The dynasty ended in 907 when a popular general, Zhu Wen, the son of impoverished gentry, forced the Tang emperor Zhaoxuan from office and proclaimed a new dynasty, the Later Liang, at Kaifeng farther down the Yellow River. Soon other military men, some from the lowest ranks of society, seized power in a number of places in the south, ushering in a half century in which China was once more divided between north and south.

BELOW
A detail of a *sancai* tomb figure of a saddled horse. China's climate and terrain were largely ill-suited to horse breeding, which meant that horses were bought from the northern Turkic peoples—often for huge quantities of precious silk. The high value of the animals reflected the fact they were needed by the Chinese to fight the mounted nomads. Figures such as this feature prominently among *mingqi* or burial goods, when in earlier times real animals had been interred. Glazed earthenware, Tang dynasty.

LEFT

The Flight of Emperor Ming Huang to Shu, an anonymous painting depicting the escape to mountainous Shu (present-day Sichuan) of the Tang emperor Ming Huang (Xuanzong) with his concubine Yang Guifei in the face of the Anlushan Rebellion in 755 (see page 95). The emperor, mounted in red robes, is on the right, leading a group of riders before the bridge; in the center, others rest in fields at the base of the mountain; and farther ahead, on the left, another group is already entering a canyon. The painting is executed in the so-called "green and blue" Tang style of landscape painting. Hanging scroll, ink and pigment on silk, Tang dynasty.

ARTS OF THE TANG

The Tang dynasty was an age of great inventiveness in the sciences, with technological developments including an improvement in water conservation through the use of waterwheels to raise water for irrigation. But it is for the arts that the Tang remains most famous. This was partly due to the patronage and encouragement of the Tang emperors themselves, but mainly because of the greater prosperity enjoyed by the country as a whole. The increased trade across Central Asia also brought in new ideas and luxury goods from Iran and the Middle East.

Tang painting built on the achievements of the Sui dynasty. Some early Tang scroll paintings portray court scenes of ladies at work and at leisure, as in an anonymous depiction of women enjoying a banquet to musical accompaniment (see page 85). One famous scroll, attributed to Zhang Xuan (active eighth century), which only survives as a copy by the Song emperor Huizong, depicts twelve ladies preparing a long piece of newly woven white silk. Each woman is intent on her work, made evident by the rendering of her gestures and facial expression. The murals in the Tang imperial tombs, particularly those in the tomb of Princess Yongtai (see page 92), are further outstanding examples of this genre of painting.

Another artist who succeeded perfectly in capturing people's expressions in a fleeting moment was Zhou Fang (ca. 730–800). His *Ladies Playing Double Sixes* depicts four figures in close-up playing a game similar to backgammon. The two players show intense concentration on their game, while of the two onlookers, one is fascinated, while the other's thoughts are clearly elsewhere.

It was said of the poet and painter Wang Wei (701–761) that his poetry contains painting and his painting poetry. Of his paintings that have survived the best known are his

LEFT
A pair of silver scissors illustrates techniques introduced to Tang China by craftsmen from Central Asia and the Near East. It is made from beaten metal, rather than casting, and engraved with floral and bird motifs.

landscapes, but a portrait of the Han-dynasty scholar Fu Sheng attributed to Wang also ranks him among the great figurative artists of the Tang. The painting expresses the Confucian love of learning and the desire to transmit the teachings of the ancients to others. It is also a portrait of the ideal teacher.

It is as a great poet that Wang Wei is most celebrated, and indeed the Tang was perhaps the finest age of Chinese poetry—*The Complete Poems of the Tang* contains nearly 50,000 poems by more than 2,000 different poets. The poets of the time had broken free from conventional themes and wrote poetry on every aspect of natural and human life. Instead of confining their interest to people of their own literate class they wrote about every stratum of society, including the common people. There were poems about soldiers, peasants, merchants, artisans, carters, and even nuns. Such a

ABOVE
A silk panel embroidered with ducks and flowers, from cave no.17 at Mogao near Dunhuang, Gansu province. It is a particularly fine example of the scrolling foliage motifs that were popular during the Tang and were used as decoration for centuries afterward. Silk and silver thread on silk, Tang dynasty, 9th–10th century.

ABOVE
A gold wine cup on a lotus-flower base and decorated with incised scenes of musicians and huntsmen. This style of multisided drinking vessel was popular during the Tang period.

wide range of subject matter had never been seen in poetry before and it bore witness to a more liberal social atmosphere under the Tang, with many poems displaying a marked humanitarian flavor.

THREE-DIMENSIONAL MASTERPIECES

Most Tang sculpture is to be found in Buddhist grottoes such as those of Dunhuang and Dazu (see pages 74–77), but the biggest Buddha of all is at Leshan in Sichuan (see page 70). Carved into a cliff on the bank of the Min River and situated near the confluence of three rivers, the site was chosen partly because the treacherous currents had caused the deaths of many boatmen in the area and it was thought that the presence of Maitreya (Mile Fo), the popular Buddha of the future, would save lives and bring merit to the donors. Work began at the behest of a famous monk of the region in 713 and the sculpture was completed ninety years later and painted. With a height of 234 ft (71 m) and width at the shoulders of 78 ft (24 m), it is the world's largest seated Buddha.

During the Tang period new techniques were invented in pottery and porcelain (see pages 139–143), as well as in weaving and dyeing, while fine gold and silver objects were produced using techniques learned from the Iranians such as chasing, punching, and *repoussé*. According to Tang records there were fourteen different ways of working gold to make vessels, jewelry, and ornaments. Two major hoards of gold and silver have come to light in recent decades. One was discovered buried in a cave not far from the Tang capital Chang'an (Xi'an) in 1970 and comprised over two hundred items, including wine cups and other eating and drinking utensils, incense burners, and pomanders. Many were elaborately yet judiciously decorated with plants, real and mythical animals, human figures, and so on. They were mostly made at the height of Tang prosperity, but a good number show foreign influence and some were clearly imported.

The second hoard was discovered more recently in Famensi Buddhist monastery at Baoji in Shaanxi province, also not very far from Chang'an. The monastery's pagoda had collapsed and needed to be rebuilt, and workmen clearing the debris discovered a cellar that had been forgotten for centuries. For many years, on the Buddha's birthday, Tang rulers gave a precious gift to the monastery, which the monks stored in the cellar. The Famensi hoard belongs to a somewhat later period of the Tang and, while smaller than the first hoard, its treasures show even more skill and artistic refinement, and rather less influence from imported styles.

Bronze figurines of the Tang include some from outside China proper, such as dancers from what is now Tashkent in Central Asia performing their native *huteng* dance, which was among the foreign dances then popular in the Chinese capital.

RIGHT
Controlling the glazes used in *sancai* ware was a skilled and difficult task; often, however, Tang potters clearly delighted in the variety of colors and patterns that arose from allowing the glazes to run together. On this large jar with dragon-headed handles, the potter has exploited the fluidity to particularly striking effect.

五

CHAPTER FIVE

A SOUTHWARD SHIFT

907 – 1279 CE

THE AGE OF
THE SONG

飛肅似怜毛羽貴俳佪如飽稻粱心
絢膺紺趾誠端雅爲賦新篇安試唫

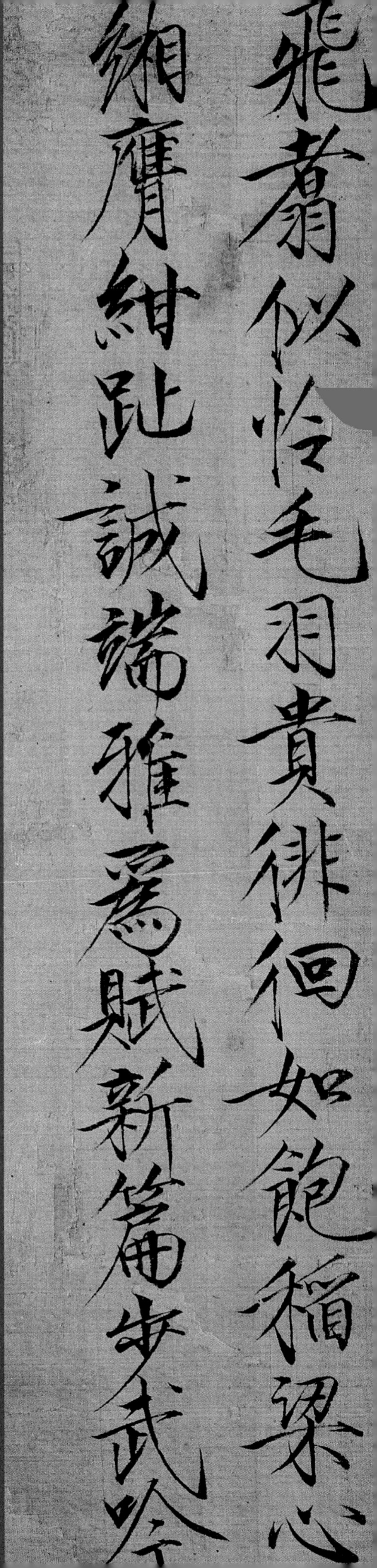

辽

WARRIORS IN THE NORTH

The Liao and Jurchen Jin, 907–1234 CE

BELOW
The Qiyun ("Cloud-Reaching") pagoda at the White Horse monastery near Luoyang, Henan province, was built in 1125 under the rule of the Jurchen Jin (see page 109). Like the Liao, another warrior people that occupied parts of northern China, the Jin adopted Chinese culture and styles.

辽 Following the fall of the Tang dynasty, China was again divided among regional kingdoms in north and south. In the north, the first of the Five Dynasties (907–960) was founded when Zhu Wen set up the Later Liang dynasty in 907, after forcing the last Tang emperor to abdicate (Zhu subsequently had him murdered). There followed about half a century of almost continuous warfare, in which five regimes succeeded each other in relatively swift succession: the Later Liang (907–923), Later Tang (923–935), Later Jin (936–947), Later Han (947–951), and Later Zhou (951–960). This second period of disunion was a lingering consequence of the Anlushan Rebellion of the mid-750s (see page 95), which encouraged factions within the Tang army, often led by men of foreign origin, to attempt to seize control of the country. Each of these kingdoms resorted to extreme measures to finance their armies, erecting customs barriers at their frontiers and exacting unreasonable taxes from the peasants. It was left to the last of them, the Later Zhou, to adopt a policy of nonaggression and attend to the recovery of the economy. The Later Zhou was overthrown in 960 by another military leader, Zhao Kuangyin, who established the Song dynasty in Kaifeng (see page 114).

Meanwhile, in the south, there were no fewer than nine states within the same time span. These nine and a small northern state in what is now Shanxi province constitute what are known as the "Ten Kingdoms." On the whole they were less bellicose and more prosperous than the northern "dynasties." It was once again the Song who overthrew the last of these.

LORDS OF CATHAY: THE LIAO

The Song established a united empire, but it was smaller than the Tang and in the north not all Chinese came under Song rule. In 924 the Khitans (Qidan), a warrior people from the Siramuren valley in Manchuria, launched an offensive against the Tangut state of Xia to the west in order to secure their rear, and then struck southward into China and occupied what is now Beijing ("Northern Capital"), which they named

Nanjing, "Southern Capital" (not to be confused with the other city farther south of the same name). The Khitans named their expanding empire the Liao (the Chinese for the Siramuren region) and occupied large swathes of Manchuria, Mongolia, and north China, at times even penetrating as far south as Kaifeng, the Song capital, and into large areas of Hebei and Shanxi. They coexisted alongside the Song, with whom in 1004 they signed a peace treaty whereby the Song recognized Liao territories and promised to pay them an annual tribute of many ounces of silver and rolls of silk. This tribute was doubled in 1042 when the Liao promised to help the Song deal with the Tanguts, another northern warrior people who had founded a state on the Chinese model.

Liao influence spread even farther. Japan in the east and Russia in the west had at least peripheral contact with the Liao as the rulers of parts of China. It is from "Khitan" that *Kitai*, the Russian for "China," is derived, as are "Cathay" and other old European names for China.

Over time the rulers of Liao became ever more influenced by the Han Chinese economy and culture, which continued to prosper even in the areas of China they controlled. This was because the Liao carried out a policy of allowing the the Han under their rule virtual self-government based on Tang administrative practice, while ruling their own people

BELOW
A flourishing Buddhist culture under the Liao and Jin produced works of striking realism such as this figure of the *arhat* Tamrabhadra. *Arhats* (Chinese *luohan*), disciples of the Buddha who also gained enlightenment, were popular subjects of Buddhist art. Glazed earthenware, Liao–Jin period.

according to their own traditions. In spite of their nomadic origins, the Khitans had already become involved in agriculture before their occupation of northern China, as well as silk weaving, pottery, iron foundries, and other industrial processes. The Liao dynasty was a period in which handicrafts of all kinds flourished and many fine architectural and sculptural masterpieces were created.

Eventually the Liao appetite for conquest waned and the state became more and more defensive. However, their enmity toward the Song dynasty did not entirely end, especially as the Song regarded them as their major enemy in the north, and the Liao continued to oppress other tribal groups under their control, in particular the Jurchens of northern Manchuria.

THE DYNASTY OF GOLD: JURCHEN JIN

The Jurchens, a warlike Tungusic people of Heilongjiang, the most northerly Manchurian province, were ancestors of the Manchus who later ruled China as the Qing dynasty (1644–1911; see Chapter Seven). In 1115 the chief of the Jurchens had founded a dynasty which he named Jin ("Gold") because of deposits of precious metal that were present in the Jurchen homeland. Twelve years later, in 1125, the Jurchen allied with the Song and together they conquered their common enemy, the Liao. But within two years the Jurchens had turned on their Chinese allies, ousted the Song from Kaifeng, and overrun all of northern China. They also conquered Manchuria and most of Mongolia.

Like the Khitans, the Jurchen Jin created a system of self-governing "empires" in areas occupied by the Chinese, under Chinese governors. However, as had happened under the Liao dynasty, the administration and culture of the entire Jin state became increasingly sinified, and the Jurchens themselves largely assimilated with the Han majority. However, the rivalry with the Song—now based in the southern city of Hangzhou in Zhejiang province—remained, and in 1153 the Jurchens transferred their capital from Harbin to Beijing and launched a series of mostly unsuccessful offensives against the south. However, the Southern Song held out and in 1234 the Jurchen Jin state was overrun by the most fearsome northern warriors of all: the Mongols.

OPPOSITE
A winged, openwork crown unearthed from the tomb of a princess at Zhelimu, the site of a Liao royal cemetery in Inner Mongolia. It bears designs including phoenixes, and is surmounted by the figure of a deity. Gilded silver, Liao dynasty, dated 1018.

BELOW
In much of their art the Liao adhered to traditional Chinese iconography. This box recalls Buddhist reliquaries of the Tang, and its incised and *repoussé* designs include Buddhist motifs such as *apsaras* (female spirits) dancing amid clouds that recall 9th-century Tang paintings at Dunhuang. Partly gilded silver, Liao dynasty, dated 1024.

CALLIGRAPHY

The Art of Writing

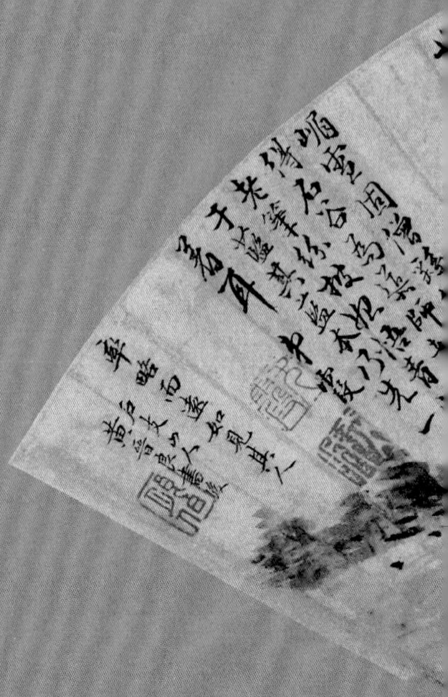

The art of calligraphy was important from early on in Chinese history. It arose from the nature of the Chinese script, including the variety of forms among the many thousands of characters that are used. Many of the earliest Chinese characters were pictograms, and some present-day characters are direct descendants of them, such as the words for horse, person, and tree. This meant that from the earliest times a link existed between calligraphy and painting. Later characters included combinations of two pictograms, such as the sun and the moon combining to make the word *ming* ("bright"). A phonetic element was also introduced: for example, in Chinese the word for "horse" is *ma* and the character for "horse" is used to represent the sound "*ma*" in a range of other words. Pronounced with a different tone, *ma* also means "mother," which is written with the character for "horse" plus the character for "woman," to indicate the sense. Naturally the structure of Chinese characters is not always so simple, but the multitude of their shapes makes them an ideal subject for calligraphic art.

THE FOUR TREASURES

The brushes, paper, ink, and stone used in calligraphy are known as "the Four Treasures of the Artist's Study." The main writing instrument until quite recently was the brush, which was used as long ago as the Neolithic period—the designs on the pottery of the Yangshao culture (see Chapter One) were painted with a brush. In the Bronze-Age Shang dynasty, characters on the oracle bones used in divination (see page 21) were engraved, but traces of vermilion within some of the characters show that in some cases they had first been written with a brush. The earliest surviving writing brush, dating from the Warring States period, was made of bamboo with a tuft of rabbit hair. Later brushes were differentiated into types by using different animal hairs.

Control of the brush is the chief discipline in the practice of calligraphy. It determines the strength, width, and direction of the stroke, and whether the full brush or only the tip is required. The brush is held vertically, but there are no strict rules as to which fingers are used.

On the oracle bones the direction of the writing depended on the shape of the bones, but in later ages it was the Chinese habit to write in vertical columns, starting at

ABOVE
A fan painted with a landscape and inscription in the style of the Yuan-dynasty *literati* artist and calligrapher Ni Zan (1301–1374) by Wang Hui (1632–1717). One of the Four Masters of the Late Yuan, Ni Zan was highly praised for his calligraphy and landscapes, which he himself dismissed as mere "ink play."

RIGHT
A page from an album of seals by Qian Weicheng (1720–1772), illustrating running script and (in red) seal script. Ink and pigment on paper, Qing dynasty, reign of Qianlong (1736–1795).

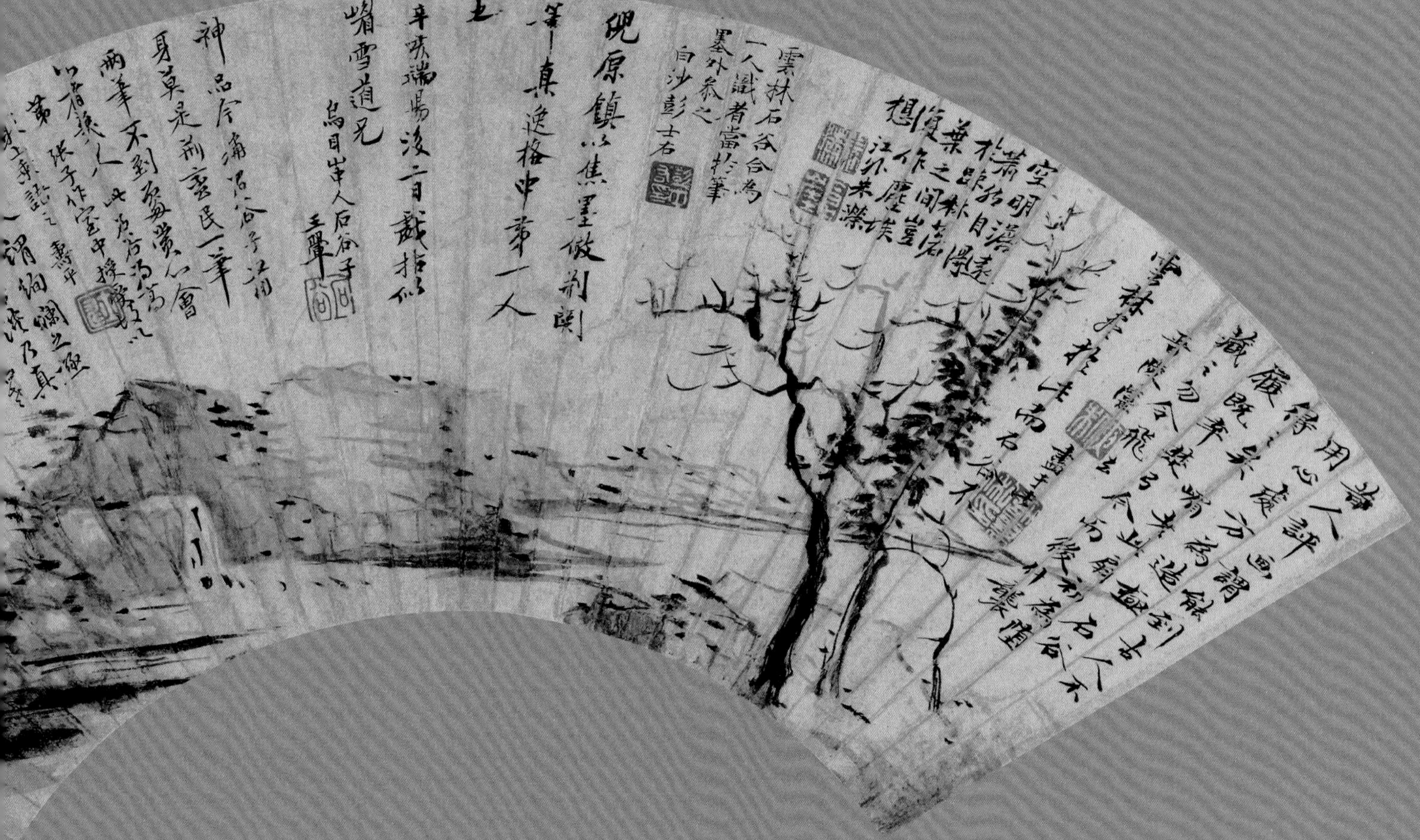

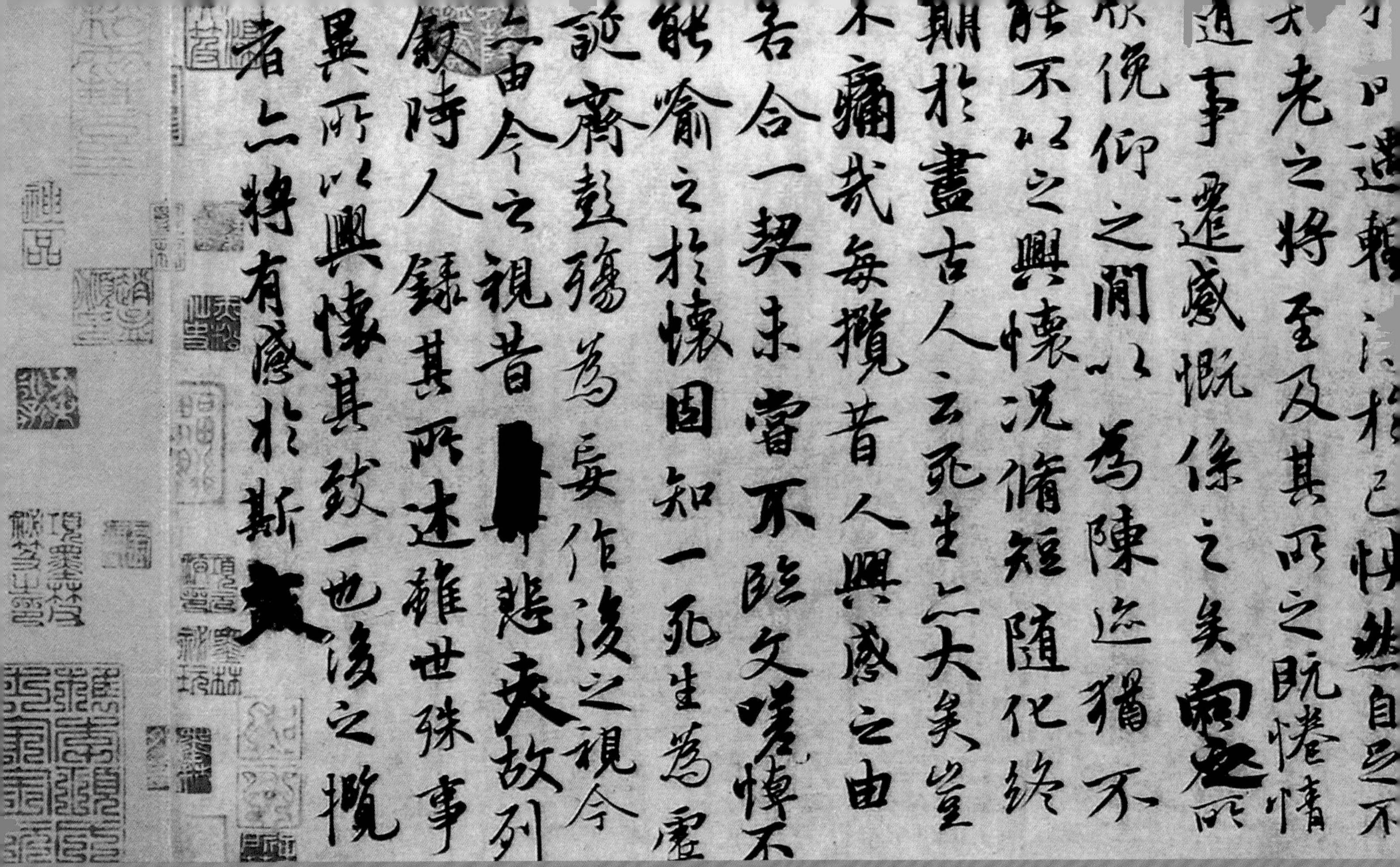

ABOVE

An extract from *The Preface to the Orchid Pavilion Collection* (353 CE) by the Jin-dynasty artist Wang Xizhi (303–361), one of the great masterpieces of Chinese calligraphy. Written in a single rapid creative burst in Wang's uniquely dynamic form of running script, the *Preface* was the introduction to a collection of works by his circle of *literati* friends. It ensured Wang's fame as China's most admired calligraphic artist, and earned him the epithet "Sacred Calligrapher." The Tang emperor Taizong collected Wang's works, and the Ming scholar Li Rihua ranked them as the most prized of all objects of beauty for discriminating *literati*.

the top of the right-hand column. This was probably because the written surface was most often strips of wood or bamboo. If horizontal writing were required, such as for an inscription above a door, the characters would be written from right to left, as if the vertical columns were reduced to one character per line. It is only in modern times, under Western influence, that horizontal writing with lines running from left to right has been adopted.

As an alternative to wooden strips, silk fabric was used as a writing medium, but after the invention of paper in the Eastern Han dynasty, this was the chosen material because of the variety of textures it could provide, ranging from rough to smooth. Most Chinese paintings and calligraphy are in scroll form and can range from quite small to several meters long. Valuable scrolls are usually kept locked away out of the light and are only brought out on special occasions.

Chinese ink is made of lampblack and a kind of glue, which is first mixed into a paste and then put into a mold and dried. The resulting ink cake must be ground on a stone and mixed with water before use. The stone on which the ink is rubbed is often a work of art in its own right.

STYLES OF WRITING

The technical and aesthetic demands of calligraphy made it inevitable that different styles of writing developed, ranging from the archaic to the modern and from the

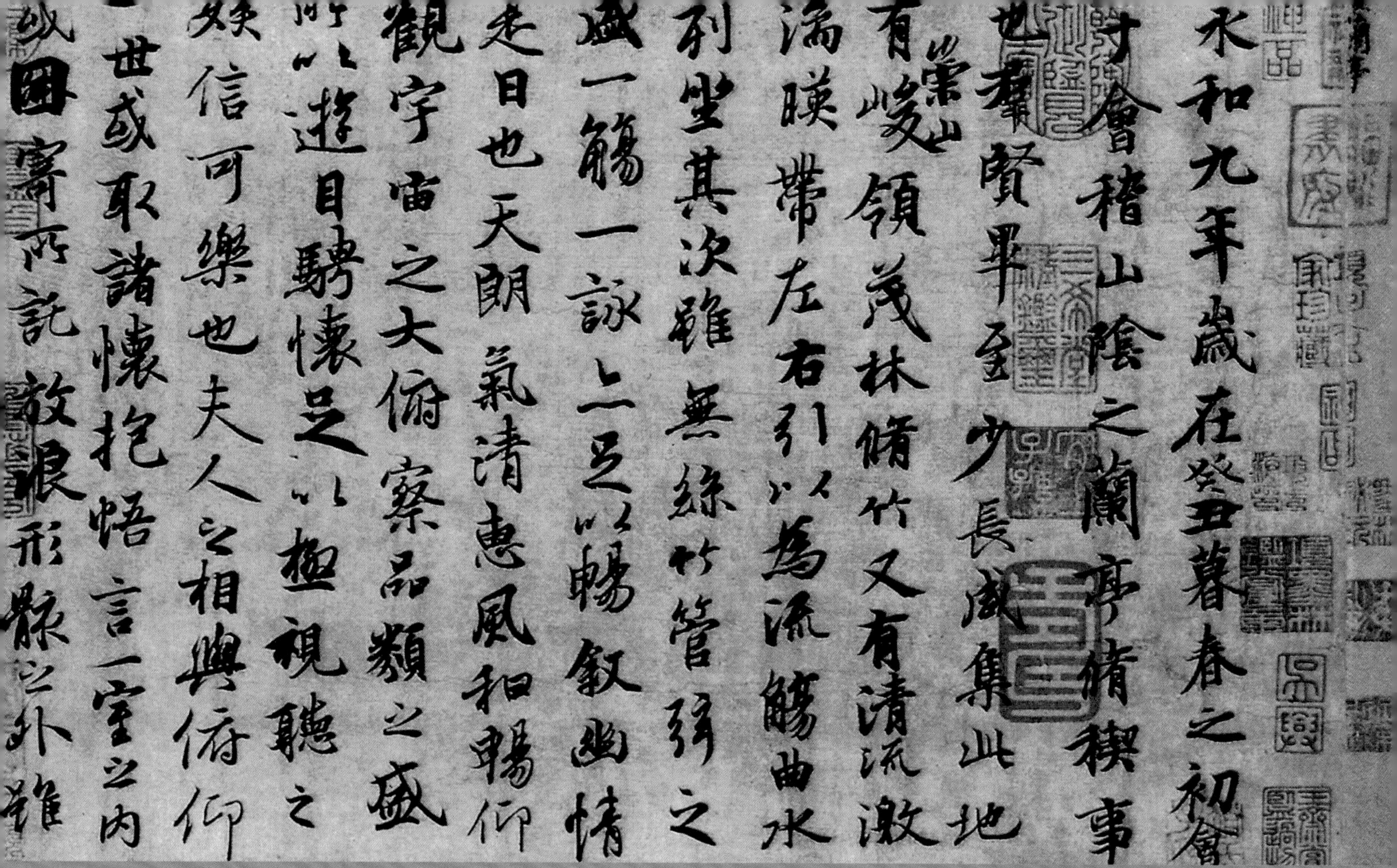

"regular" style in which each brush stroke of a character is distinct, to the "cursive" or "grass" script, in which the individual character merely hints at its original regular form, and which is in effect a kind of Chinese shorthand. Between these two is the "running" style, in which the main form of the character is intact but conventional shortcuts in its execution give it a freedom of style absent in regular characters. This style is the one favored by most contemporary Chinese writers and is often used in correspondence.

Chinese calligraphers would sometimes favor an ancient form of script based on a pre-Han style known as "seal script," because it is frequently used by carvers of official or individual seals. Many famous calligraphers and artists carved their own or their friends' seals. These are often highly prized, and the seal still serves as a signature to a painting or a document. Some paintings have multiple seals on them, some applied by the artist, others added by the owners of the pictures. In every dynasty there have been master calligraphers in each or all of these main styles.

BELOW
The calligrapher's tools are often exquisite objects in themselves, such as this porcelain-handled brush decorated with floral scrolls with dragons in two white panels. White porcelain with underglaze blue, Ming dynasty, dated from the inscription on the handle to the reign of Wanli (1573–1620).

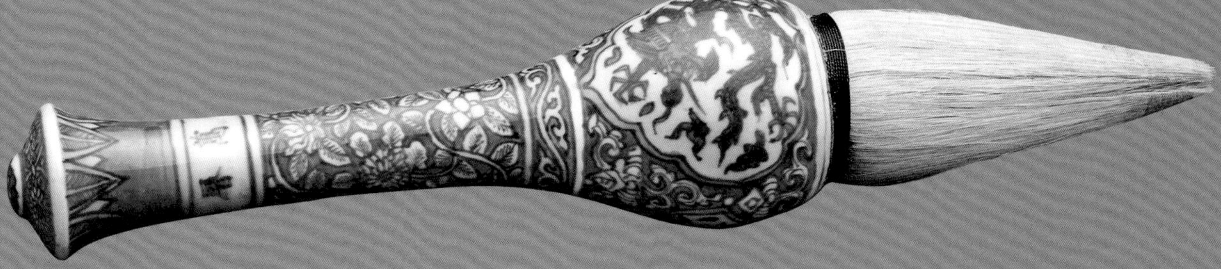

宋

LORDS OF KAIFENG

The Northern Song (960–1126)

BELOW
A blue-green celadon jug with a double phoenix-headed spout and bearing incised floral decoration characteristic of the early Song kilns at Yaozhou, Shaanxi. The deeply incised lines permit an attractive contrast between lighter areas of relief and darker areas where glaze has accumulated over several firings. Northern Song, early 11th century.

宋 In 960 Zhao Kuangyin, a military leader of the Later Zhou, one of the northern "Five Dynasties" (see page 106), staged a rebellion and founded the Song dynasty in Kaifeng, taking the name of Emperor Taizu (ruled 960–976). The first period of the Song dynasty (960–1126) is now often called the Northern Song, because in 1126 the north of China was overrun by the Jurchen Jin armies from Manchuria, forcing the dynasty to re-establish itself at Hangzhou in the south. This second phase of the dynasty (1127–1279) is known as the Southern Song.

In 979 the second Song emperor, Taizong (976–997), completed the conquest of the last of the Ten Kingdoms of the south, the Northern Han, which lay between the Khitan state of Liao and the Song empire. However, throughout the dynasty's life the Song emperors were unable to repeat the military successes of the Tang, and never recovered the vast territories of Central and North Asia that had once been under Chinese influence or control. Instead these regions were reclaimed by native peoples such as the Khitans (Liao) and the Jurchens (Jin), who established new kingdoms to the west and north of China. Eventually the Song succumbed—along with much of Eurasia—to the mightiest and most warlike of these peoples, the Mongols.

Nevertheless the Song made great strides economically and culturally. The last of the Five Dynasties, the Northern Zhou, had already done much to restore the northern economy after nearly half a century of wars, and the Song was able to build on these achievements.

Economic development was matched by technological advances that made Song China the most industrially and scientifically advanced country in the world. Song metallurgy, printing, and weaving all surpassed previous dynasties in terms of output as well as in the sophistication of their technology. For example, the Northern Song scholar Bi Sheng (990–1051) invented the first movable type using ceramic blocks.

CULTURE DURING THE SONG

During the Song the old Chinese aristocracy that had hitherto dominated the government faded away. China was now governed by educated *literati* families living in towns, who were very different from the horse-riding, polo-playing nobility of former dynasties. Nor was so much prestige attached to feats of arms, but in contrast there was greater emphasis on intellectual pursuits, with philosophers, artists, and writers enjoying wide respect and influence at the highest levels of society. Even senior officials composed poetry to be set to music, or else devoted themselves to painting (see pages 122–127), continuing and perfecting the tradition of landscape painting established in the Tang and carried forward in the Five Dynasties. The penultimate

ABOVE

A gold cup in the form of a chrysanthemum (*ju*), or "autumn flower." The bloom became very popular as one of the "Four Honorable Plants," a symbol of nobility, along with the orchid, plum, and bamboo. In the Song dynasty 35 varieties were recorded—a number that had risen to 900 by the Ming period. Today there are more than 3,000 varieties in China alone. Northern Song dynasty, 11th century.

RIGHT
Song silkweavers developed complex techniques that resulted in striking designs such as this cover for Buddhist scriptures decorated with phoenixes, deer, and lotus flowers. Also by the time of the Song, water-powered spinning wheels enabled the rapid production of fine, regular silk thread. Embroidered silk, Northern Song dynasty, 10th–11th century.

ABOVE
A glazed, olive-green, incised earthenware bowl, characteristic of the exquisite craftsmanship and careful, subtle decoration of the Song dynasty—an era when ceramics' manufacture flourished and numerous regional centers of excellence existed. Northern Song, 12th century.

Northern Song emperor, Huizong (ruled 1101–1125), was himself a painter and calligrapher of considerable stature (see illustration pages 104–105) as well as a great collector. Unfortunately, his collection was destroyed by the Jurchen Jin when they overthrew the Northern Song in 1126. Song porcelain also reached a high level of refinement and elegance (see pages 138–143). In these and other respects China under the Song experienced a period of real renaissance.

One reason for the advance of the arts and sciences in the Song was the growth of publishing and schools, leading to higher standards of literacy and education. In the Tang, Buddhist monasteries had been the main centers for these activities, whereas in the Song more and more public and private libraries and schools were established. The biggest library of all, containing eighty thousand volumes, was in the imperial palace. Writing of all genres flourished. There was a vogue for producing volumes of notes or essays both on general and specialist subjects, one of the most famous being *Notes from Dream Stream* (*Mengxi Bitan*, 1081) by the scientist and statesman Shen Gua or Guo (1031–1095), in which he was the first to describe, among other things, the magnetic compass. A book upon which all students of Chinese architecture still base their studies was *The Methodology of Architecture* (*Yingzao Fashi*, 1103) by Li Jie, who himself designed many temples and government buildings in Kaifeng, the Northern Song capital.

AN UNEASY COEXISTENCE

The Southern Song (1127–1279)

OPPOSITE
The Baochu pagoda, north of the West Lake in Hangzhou, capital in the Southern Song era when the city was named Lin'an (Temporary Haven). Originally built between 968 and 975 during the Northern Song dynasty, the pagoda was restored several times, most recently in 1933.

BELOW
The tomb of Yue Fei (1103–1142) at Hangzhou. Chief of the Southern Song armies against the Jurchen Jin and one of China's great military heroes, Yue Fei is said to have been executed after being falsely accused. He was later rehabilitated and given this splendid tomb in recognition of his service.

When the Jurchen Jin reached Kaifeng in 1126, they packed the Song emperor, his crown prince, and the whole imperial family off northeast to their capital of Harbin in present-day Heilongjiang, Manchuria. The invaders then continued southward and sacked many towns in central and southeast China. One Song prince escaped the debacle and in 1127 he re-established the dynasty in the south at a new capital at Hangzhou in present-day Zhejiang province, with himself as emperor (Gaozong, ruled 1127–1162). From this time until its downfall in 1279 the dynasty is known as the Southern Song.

Eventually, in 1142, the Southern Song made an agreement with the Jin settling the border between them along the Huai River in Anhui province, roughly halfway between the Yellow and Yangzi rivers. The same agreement settled an annual rate of tribute to be paid by the Southern Song to the Jin, which indicates the uneasy power balance that existed between the two states. The Song vacillated between appeasement and resistance and had to fight many defensive battles to hold the Jin at bay. They were able to repossess the north only in 1234, when the Jin were being menaced by the Mongols—before whom the Song empire would itself collapse forty-five years later.

Nevertheless, in spite of the near-constant threat on its northern frontiers, the Southern Song domains prospered, building on the achievements both of earlier Song rulers and of the preceding Ten Kingdoms (906–960) that had ruled the south of China following the end of the Tang. In fact, the move of the capital to Hangzhou merely confirmed a trend that had begun under the Northern Song, which had seen the economic focus of the empire shift to the south, where commerce flourished and towns continued to grow in size and importance. Central government no longer enjoyed the degree of influence over the individual that it had before, and self-help organizations, free of strict state control, such as craft guilds were able to become established. In effect a new middle class of entrepreneurs arose, with towns brimming with shops selling all kinds of household goods and foods. There were also amusement centers where musicians, actors, and storytellers could ply their trades all the year round without being tied to religious festivals, as they had been in the past. Moneylenders, fortune-tellers, and medical practitioners also flourished.

THE NEOCONFUCIAN REVIVAL

In commercial, technological, and artistic terms the Song represented a period of innovation and progress (see pages 115–117). However, conservative thinking retained a hold on intellectual life. Many Chinese scholars blamed the disaster of 1126 on the dynasty's excessive interest in arts such as poetry and painting, while others sought

to purify China by reviving its prevalent ideology of Confucianism. This process had begun during the late Tang, partly as a reaction to the "foreign" philosophy of Buddhism. Under the Southern Song one of China's most influential philosophers, Zhu Xi (1130–1200), synthesized the ideas of previous reformers and, absorbing elements of both Buddhism and Daoism, developed a powerfully cohesive new form of Confucianism that came to be known as Neoconfucianism or the School of Li.

Li means "principle" or "reason," and according to this school everything in the world, animate and inanimate, has a *li* that sets it apart and exists independently of the object itself. Thus the *li* of boatbuilding existed before anyone ever thought of building a boat. The *li* of humankind is human nature, which Neoconfucians, like Buddhists, believe to be innately good. However, this goodness has been tarnished by worldly passions.

In cosmological terms, the *li* of the universe is *Taiji* or the Supreme Ultimate, the equivalent to the *Dao* of Daoism. To explain the physical universe Zhu Xi introduced the concept of *qi* or ("energy," "life-force"), the agency or force by which all things arise, operating through the five elements (air, earth, wood, fire, water) and the passive and active forces of *yin* and *yang*.

Consistent with Zhu Xi's theories was his idea that key human relationships also had immutable principles. This meant that any major social reform—for example, a change in the relation between a monarch and his subjects or between a husband and wife—would contradict the natural order, bringing untold disaster. Zhu Xi's ideas became the orthodox ideology during the dynasties that followed the Song, but in the twentieth century, Confucianism became regarded as an enemy of progress, even though the Neoconfucians' original aim had been to improve and stabilize society.

To promote his ideas Zhu Xi laid great stress on the ancient Confucian classics known as the Four Books: *The Analects* of Confucius, *The Book of Mencius*, *The Doctrine of the Mean*, and *The Great Learning*. These became basic reading for all scholars aspiring to pass the examinations that would qualify them for government service, and they remained so for the next 700 years.

ABOVE
A miniature bucket or cauldron inlaid with an intricate design resembling motifs of the ancient Shang and Zhou dynasties. Bronze with gold and silver inlay, Song dynasty.

OPPOSITE
This peacock on a lotus base was discovered in the Tang-dynasty Qianxun pagoda near Dali city, Yunnan province, in the south of China. In this area Buddhism escaped the worst of the persecutions of the late Tang. Gilded silver with inlaid crystal, Southern Song dynasty.

PAINTING OF THE SONG

Artists and Emperors

Short though it was, the Five Dynasties period (907–960) brought about a major breakthrough in the field of the arts, and especially painting. Artists of the era were thought of as pioneers of a new kind of art which sought to capture not only a resemblance to the subject but also something more—the spirit of the subject and the soul of the painter himself. One artist of the period wrote: "Resemblance reproduces the formal aspect of things but neglects their spirit. Truth shows the essence and spirit in its perfection."

The reasons for the developments in painting under the Five Dynasties are not straightforward, but one factor was the splitting of China into smaller, unstable units, which had led educated men who in previous dynasties might have entered government service to abandon their plans to serve their emperor or their country and transfer their energies elsewhere. Many of these *literati* were unemployed and used their copious leisure time to explore the world of nature, which had been so brilliantly portrayed by Tang-dynasty poets such as Wang Wei and Meng Haoran. It was during the Five Dynasties that the fashion for landscape painting was established, which

OPPOSITE
Along the Riverbank at Dusk by Dong Yuan (active 930s–960s). Travellers approach a tavern, right, on a tranquil spring evening. Dong's typical blue-and-green palette was renowned, as were his mountains rendered with a hemp-fiber brush. Hanging scroll, ink and color on silk.

RIGHT
Travelling among Mountains and Streams by Fan Kuan (active 990–1030). The group follows a path in the foreground toward a stream. The towering mountains dominate the scene, emphasizing the comparative insignificance of humankind. Hanging scroll, ink and color on silk.

ABOVE
Thick Mist with River and Mountains (detail) by Mi Fei (1051–1107) is typical of his highly influential impressionistic and economical style. Handscroll, ink on paper.

was carried to its full maturity during the Song dynasty. Very few works by Five Dynasties artists are extant, but the painters of the Song took their predecessors' ideas further and created a brilliant legacy of art, much of which has survived.

The life of the painter Dong Yuan (active 930s–960s), who was also a Buddhist monk, spans the Five Dynasties and early Northern Song periods. His work displays the ethos of Song artists, who no longer give the impression of painting literally from nature, but express their own concept of nature in an idealized form. This is seen to good effect in works by Dong such as *Along the Riverbank at Dusk*, which depicts travellers in a mountainous landscape approaching the end of a day's journey in the artist's characteristic blue-green palette (see page 123). Some works are more contemplative, and the natural scene appears tranquil and even bucolic, while other artists are attracted to the power of wind and water, their works showing nature in constant flux.

Another Northern Song painter, Fan Kuan (active 990–1030), drew inspiration from Daoism, and lived a hermit's life in the mountains. In his most famous surviving painting, *Travelling among Mountains and Streams* (see page 122), a small party of travellers are dwarfed by a huge rock-face towering above them, thus underlining the relationship between humankind and the world they inhabit. Although a somewhat austere painter, Fan Kuan was a superb artist. He invented a technique of using dots and small brush strokes to give the impression of light playing over large surfaces.

Even more inventive was Mi Fei (or Mi Fu, 1051–1107), a government official and an individualist who painted purely for his own pleasure, producing landscapes simply as the spirit moved him. His works, which include such masterpieces as *Thick Mist with River and Mountains* and *Spring Mountains and Pine Trees*, might show, for example, a group of conical mountains emerging from a blanket of white mist with groups of trees in the

宿雨清畿甸
朝陽麗帝城
豐年人樂業
壠上踏歌行

foreground. The pictures are often quite impressionistic, with the whole scene reduced to a few basic elements, executed with the utmost economy. His style had a profound influence on the landscapes of the Southern Song.

The Northern Song dynasty also favored paintings of flowers, birds, and animals. The emperor Huizong (1101–1125) was a master of this subject and some of his paintings have survived, though many were destroyed during the Jin conquest of 1126. His *Five-Colored Parakeet*, depicting the bird perched on a branch of plum blossom, is a masterpiece of composition as well as of brush control (see illustration pages 104–105). Huizong headed an academy of painting in Kaifeng, following the precedent set by the ill-fated Tang emperor Xuanzong. This academy accepted as members some of the most accomplished painters of the age, though as time went by it became more conservative in its output. It was ransacked and its members either exiled or dispersed by the Jin, but it was restored by the Southern Song soon after the flight to Hangzhou.

OPPOSITE
Willows and Distant Mountains by the Southern Song artist Ma Yuan. Ma's lyrical and expressive landscapes influenced many later painters, and the characteristic asymmetry of his composition earned him the nickname "One-Corner Ma." Ink and watercolor on silk.

CHAN: THE ART OF ENLIGHTENMENT

While the Song was a period in which Buddhism as a whole was past its zenith in China, the dynasty represented a high point for art influenced by the Chan school (see pages 68–71), which believed that Buddha-nature was present in every aspect of the universe, from the smallest plant to the greatest tree, from the lowliest worm to humankind. This enormously enlarged the subject matter of painting as Chan artists sought to express in their work their belief in simplicity and a direct and unadorned "getting at the truth." Having freed themselves from extraneous thoughts and emotions through meditation, Chan painters would seek to record a visual truth about the subject with rapid, spare strokes that can produce works of marvelous spontaneity and near-abstraction. This is seen in one of the best-known Chan paintings of the Southern Song, *Six Persimmons* by Mu Qi (ca. 1210–1288), a monk in Hangzhou. Like those of other Chan artists, Mu Qi's landscapes often express the enormity of the universe. For example, his *Sunset in a Fishing Village* depicts a tiny fisherman in a landscape of mist-clad mountains, emphasizing the insignificance of human beings against nature.

Mu Qi and other Chan painters of the Song, such as Ma Yuan (ca. 1160–1225) and Yu Jian (active ca. 1250) had a profound effect on subsequent Chinese art history, as well as on art in Japan, where Chan became established as Zen.

BELOW
One of the most famous Song-dynasty paintings, *Six Persimmons* by Mu Qi (ca. 1210–1288), implies a swiftly executed style, while its use of line and wash with an innovative arrangement of subject matter is characteristic of works by Chan artists.

六

CHAPTER SIX

CONQUEST AND AUTOCRACY

1279–1644

THE YUAN AND MING

THE COMING OF THE KHANS

The Yuan Dynasty, 1279–1368

For decades the Southern Song managed to hold off the threat from the Mongols to the north, assisted by their control of southern China's waterways. Following the example of the Jurchen Jin, whom they had conquered in 1234, the Mongols recruited Chinese experts to achieve their goal of occupying the rest of China; these experts helped the Mongols to build a fleet which in 1273 captured the important city of Xiangyang. This was the beginning of the end for the Song, and the Mongol conquest was completed in 1279. The Mongol leader, Khubilai Khan (ruled 1279–1294) established a new dynasty, the Yuan, which was to rule China for the best part of the next hundred years.

In this period China was not only ruled by a foreign regime—the first time that non-Han people had ruled the whole of China—but constituted only one province in an empire that had come to occupy a vast swathe of the Eurasian continent. In 1206 the Mongol chieftain Temujin (ca. 1150/ca. 1160–1227) had united the tribes of the Mongolian grasslands into a powerful fighting force and earned the title by which he is generally known: Jinghis or Genghis Khan ("Universal Ruler"). He then led his army westward into Asia, conquering a great part of it. Deeply ingrained in the Mongols'

BELOW
Bamboo Groves in Mist and Rain by Guan Daosheng (1262–1319), one of the most distinguished female artists and calligraphers of the period. Her paintings of bamboo expressed the idea of strength in adversity (see page 135). Handscroll; ink on paper, dated 1308.

psyche was the idea that city-dwellers were somehow inferior to the nomadic peoples of the steppes. Hence, while he generally spared the rulers who surrendered to him, Jinghis Khan sometimes slaughtered the inhabitants of whole cities that offered resistance, as happened several times during the conquest of China. The Mongol armies even reached as far west as Europe, and for a time incorporated Hungary and Poland into their empire, making it the largest area of the world ever ruled by a single regime.

Under Jinghis Khan's successor Ogodai, the Mongols' policy was modified. They interfered less in the administration of the territories that had surrendered to them, and relied more on local taxation than captured booty to support their armies. They also recruited local experts, so when Jinghis Khan's grandson, Khubilai Khan, established Mongol rule in China he started using Khitan and Jurchen experts who had served the Liao and Jin dynasties, to help the Mongols exploit China's wealth. Of particular service to him was Yelü Qucai, a former Khitan aristocrat, who restored the Chinese fiscal system and was appointed governor of North China.

THE JEWEL IN THE MONGOL CROWN

China was undoubtedly the Mongols' biggest prize and they began to think of it as the center of their empire. Under Khubilai Khan they moved their capital from Mongolia to Dadu (Beijing), which they called Khanbalik, and gave their regime the Chinese name Yuan after a term in the Chinese classic *Book of Changes* (*Yijing*) as though they were

ABOVE
Khubilai Khan, grandson of Jinghis Khan and first emperor (1268–1294) of the Yuan dynasty. Ink and paint on silk, from an album of portraits of eight Yuan rulers, 14th century.

just another Chinese dynasty. Yet the Mongols still thought it necessary to execute a policy of racial discrimination. They divided the population into categories based on ethnicity, with preference given to ethnic groups in the order in which they submitted to Mongol rule. The major categories they recognized were: the Mongols and other nomadic tribes, who were usually given preference; the "Colored Eyes," those who were neither Mongol nor Chinese; and lastly the Han, who included not only the Chinese, but also sinicized Khitans, Jurchens, and so on. Within these main categories there were dozens of subgroups among the nomadic tribes, and also among the "Colored Eyes," including for example Turks, Tibetans, Iranians, and Russians. Social mobility among the Han was severely restricted.

The Mongols occupied China when it was in the midst of an economic expansion, and this continued, though at a slower pace, after the conquest. One of the measures that the Yuan introduced was the nationwide use of paper money, which had first appeared during the Song, but only in a piecemeal way. One of the reasons for this was the Yuans' excessive use of silver to finance their trade with Central and Western Asia, which led to a shortage of silver coins. Unfortunately for the Yuan economy, the paper money later suffered from serious inflation.

During the Yuan dynasty people made their way to China from many different parts of the world. Also many Chinese settled in Southeast and Southern Asia, establishing overseas colonies of Chinese merchants and craftsmen. It was during the Yuan that the Venetian traveller Marco Polo (1254–1324) supposedly visited China, though this has been disputed. A famous Arab traveller, Ibn Battuta (1304–ca. 1370), certainly did go to Yuan China and his reports included an even more interesting account than Polo's. Among other things Ibn Battuta wrote about China's technical achievements, including hydraulic machines, boat construction, and so on, as well as reporting the widespread use of coal for heating and industrial purposes.

During the Yuan there was an increase in seagoing trade and, as observed by Ibn Battuta, boatbuilding flourished. The Yuan dynasty used Chinese ships and personnel for their expeditions to Southeast Asia and also for their ill-fated military expedition to Japan, which was defeated by a hurricane that the Japanese named the "divine wind" (*kamikaze*). The Yuan also spent ten years digging a canal linking the Yangzi River with their capital at Dadu (Beijing), which connected to the existing Grand Canal (see pages 80–82) and to Hangzhou.

The Yuan dynasty is not noted for its encouragement of philosophical speculation, and the progress in this field during the Southern Song was not continued. The Chinese scholar–gentry, traditional keepers of Chinese philosophical values, were low down the Yuan hierarchy. However, the work of the Neoconfucian Zhu Xi (see page 121) was translated into Mongolian. The Mongols also encouraged the entry of Islam into China, and Muslim communities were established in many provinces. The construction of the Yuan palace in Dadu (Beijing) was entrusted to a Muslim architect and many mosques were built to cater for the Muslim minority.

The Mongols valued the technicians and craftsmen in the lands they conquered, and they either encouraged or coerced some Chinese artisans to settle in Mongolia. Guo Shoujing (1231–1316), a polymath engineer, mathematician, and astronomer, was entrusted with the regulation of China's rivers and canals, and was later put in charge of the reform of the calendar. He constructed Lake Kunming in Beijing as a reservoir, and nearly three centuries before the Gregorian calendar was devised in Europe, he correctly calculated the solar year to be 365.2425 days long.

BELOW
A blue-and-white wine jar with a design of fishes and aquatic plants. White porcelain with underglaze blue first appeared in China between ca. 1325 and 1350, soon after cobalt oxide pigment was first imported from the Middle East. This very fine jar is unusual in that it is painted as a single, 360-degree image; it shows four fishes with names that constitute a rebus of the phrase "honest and incorruptible." Yuan dynasty, 14th century.

ARTS UNDER THE YUAN

Well before the Mongols occupied China, they possessed highly esteemed Chinese ceramics and silks, which they obtained through trade and barter, and after the fall of the Song their continued manufacture was encouraged. The Yuan dynasty is noted for its ceramics (see pages 138–143), and painting also continued to flourish during the period. The most versatile and accomplished painter and calligrapher of the Yuan era was Zhao Mengfu (1254–1322), whose landscapes, portraits, and horse paintings all display his skill and

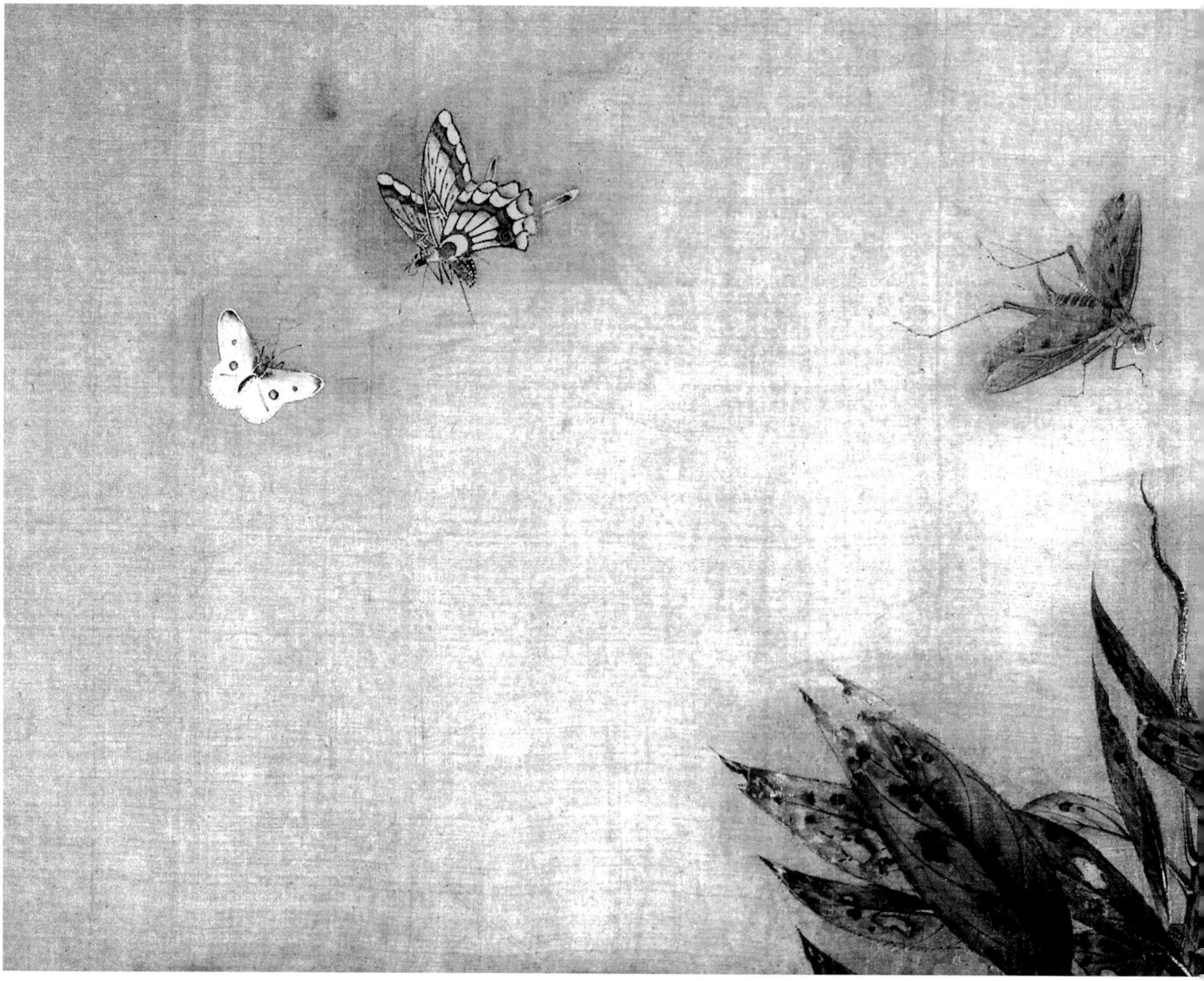

ABOVE
Fascination of Nature (1321) by Xie Chufang (detail) is an exquisitely accurate representation of nature that also, in its depiction of beauty alongside creatures preying on one another, expresses the situation in which many Chinese *literati* found themselves under Mongol rule—whether to work for the new regime and survive, or to retain fealty to the old dynasty and starve.

inventiveness. He was inspired by Tang works but also espoused the landscape styles of the Song-dynasty *literati* painters. One of his paintings, entitled *The Round Pear*, depicts a group of men playing a Chinese form of football. Zhao was the husband of Guan Daosheng, another Yuan painter of note (see below).

Of the later Yuan painters, Ni Zan (1301–1374) produced landscapes with large stretches of water, distant hills, and nearby trees. His works exude tranquillity and were the inspiration of the *literati* painters of the later Ming and Qing dynasties (see pages 110–111). Ni Zan spent the last twenty years of his life either in a houseboat on Lake Tai or wandering about the countryside, living the life of a Daoist ascetic and avoiding the attentions of officials. Ni Zan's dilemma was one that confronted other artists: whether to work for the Mongols and prosper but risk being viewed as a traitor, or remain loyal to the fallen dynasty and face penury and even persecution. *Fascination of Nature* by Xie

Chufang (active late 1200s–early 1300s) is a beautiful depiction of animals and insects hunting each other among flowers; but inscriptions added to the work explain that the beauty of nature masks disorder and a struggle for survival, an allusion to China under the Yuan. The painting belongs to a genre called *caochong* ("plants and insects"), which originated late in the Northern Song: Chinese painters working under the Mongols sometimes consciously recalled the glorious past by reviving styles of the former era.

Other Yuan artists expressed a form of stoic resignation in their work. The calligrapher, poet, and painter Guan Daosheng (1262–1319) was renowned for her paintings of bamboo (see pages 130–131), a favorite subject of Chinese artists. Because it is a plant that bends in rough weather but does not break, the bamboo was admired for possessing qualities that it was believed would stand all people—not least the Chinese gentry—in good stead in troubled times.

RIGHT
This *bodhisattva* (detail) illustrates how skilled Chinese potters had become in producing fine, pure white, hard-paste porcelain. White porcelain, a hard and translucent ware fired at very high temperatures, was first developed during the Han and was perfected by the time of the Northern Song. Yuan dynasty, late 13th century.

ABOVE
A gold hemispherical cup with carefully incised floral designs. Yuan dynasty, 13th–14th century.

The Yuan rulers were also fond of drama. Several playwrights whose names are well known in China to this day brought Chinese drama to its peak, both musically and as literature. In Shanxi province the remains of some Yuan stages are still extant, as well as wall paintings depicting performances.

REBELLION AND DOWNFALL

After the death of Khubilai Khan, disputes over his succession undermined the Yuan dynasty. But even more important in its decline were the harsh and arbitrary laws and burdensome taxes imposed by the regime, particularly on the Chinese peasantry toward the end of the dynasty, when the Mongols were beginning to come under economic strain. This was exacerbated by the inflation of the paper money the Yuan had issued to make up the shortfall in silver.

Following great floods in the Yellow River basin, the growing resentment of the regime led many peasants to join anti-Yuan secret societies, and other anti-Yuan movements arose among salt workers and boatmen in the east. Eventually the rising hostility toward the Mongols erupted as open rebellion. A number of peasant leaders emerged, and among these was Zhu Yuanzhang, born in 1328 into a peasant family in Anhui province. During a famine in 1344 Zhu became a Buddhist monk: according to legend it was after being fired for roasting and eating one of his master's cows, but it was likely that he did so simply to survive. He later joined a messianic rebel movement, the Red Turbans, and through ability and charisma rose to become its leader. After defeating other peasant leaders who were vying for power, Zhu established a rival capital in Nanjing, and in 1368 he instituted a new dynasty, the Ming ("Brilliant"), that was to rule China until 1644.

CERAMICS OF THE TANG TO QING

Masterworks in Clay

Chinese ceramic technology made great advances from the Tang dynasty onward. In decoration Tang potters introduced the use of colored glazes on a white ground, especially the striking so-called "three-colored" (*sancai*) ware. It was used not just for pots and other vessels (see below and page 103) but also for figurines that include horses, some with riders; camels and other domestic animals; human figures (both Chinese and foreigners, many with distinctive Iranian or Central Asian features), such as civilian and military officials; tomb guardians, and so on (see pages 96 and 97). A color scheme of green and amber on a white ground was perhaps most characteristic, but other colors were also used, such as red and blue. This Tang polychrome ware was mostly produced in the period before the Anlushan Rebellion.

In addition to the glazed figures many painted figurines have survived. They include the most exquisite female examples, not only young women but also middle-aged ones, displaying the Tang fashion for somewhat plumper bodies than was common either earlier or later. There were also painted pottery figures of entertainers, including groups of musicians and dancers.

LEFT
A *sancai* (three-color) pottery wine jug in the form of a monkey holding a wineskin. Although it is categorized as *sancai*, this piece is actually produced with four colors (green, amber, and blue on white base). Tang dynasty.

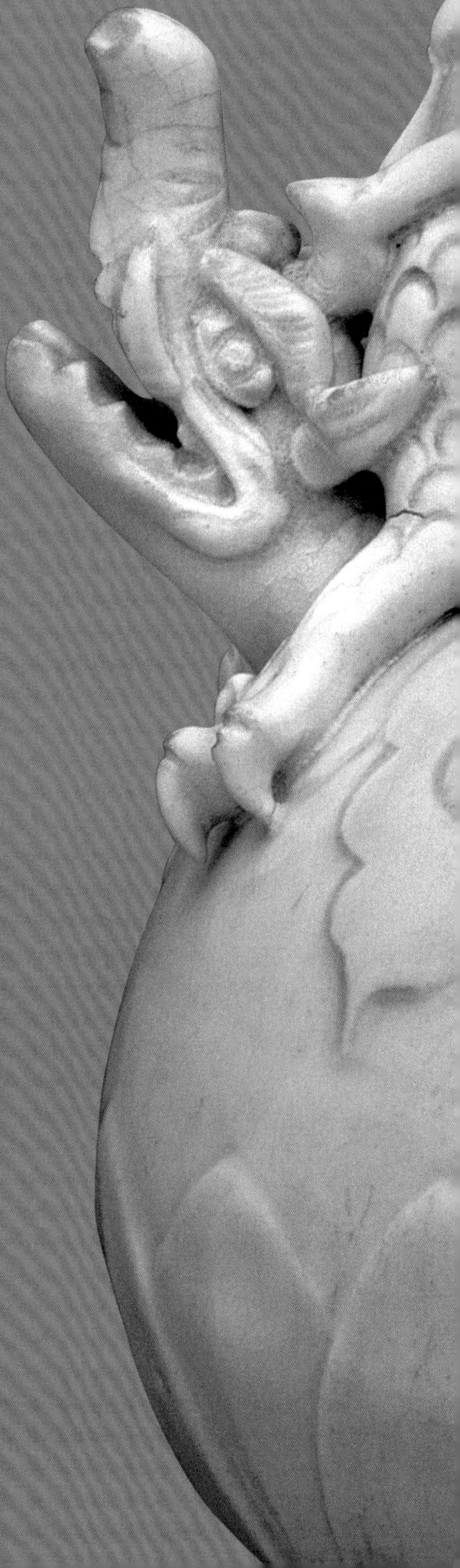

BELOW
A white ware ewer with an incised lotus flower design and an elegant handle and spout in the form of a crouching dragon. Southern Song, 13th century.

ABOVE
A *ru* ware bowl with thick, opaque pale lavender glaze covered with a faint irregular crackling. The rim is bound with a copper band. Inside the bowl a verse of poetry by the Qing emperor Qianlong was inscribed by imperial order and dated 1786. Northern Song dynasty, 12th century.

WARES OF THE SONG

Under the Song, a number of kilns in Hebei province in the north produced a range of wares for which the dynasty became famous, including *ding*, a porcelain with a fine white paste and lustrous white glaze. *Ding* ware originally followed the Tang tradition of plain white wares, but later copied designs from imported Iranian gold and silverware, often with similar foliate forms. Later still, in the Southern Song, they reverted to Chinese forms but with incised designs on the vessels reflecting the artistic fashion for natural themes, including restrained and elegant depictions of plants and animals.

Yue ware from Zhejiang province in southeast China, and later also from north Chinese kilns, typically had a blue-green or olive-green glaze which in the West is called celadon (the origin of the term is obscure). The northern celadon often surpassed the Zhejiang products in the way that their incised designs conformed to their shapes (see page 114).

Ru ware, like *guan* ware, was made for the imperial court. It was glazed but not decorated and prized for its elegant form. For these qualities it supplanted *ding* ware in imperial favor before the enforced move of the Song to the south in 1126.

Cizhou ware, also from the north, was already being produced under the Tang. A stoneware decorated with bold patterns in black or dark glaze, it is the only painted Song ceramic and continued to be manufactured into the modern period. Owing to its sturdiness and bold designs it became more akin to a folk art than a refined product for the imperial court or collectors.

LEFT
An octagonal celadon vase from Longquan, Zhejiang province. Each face has three molded panels of chrysanthemums (top and bottom), with the unglazed center panels bearing alternately a sage in clouds or another chrysanthemum spray. The panels were at some time gilt and still bear some traces of gold. Yuan dynasty, 14th century.

RIGHT
A blue-and-white dish decorated with a *qilin*, a mythical beast with horns, hooves, and scales. Despite its appearance the *qilin* is an auspicious and gentle creature, harming no life and ferocious only toward the wicked. It is associated with prosperity and its appearance is said to herald the advent of a sage. Ming dynasty, 16th–17th century.

ABOVE
A detail of a vase in the palette known as *famille rose*, which is noted for the fine detail and delicate brushwork of its designs. This aptly named *mille-fleurs* ("1,000 flowers") design, including chrysanthemums, peonies, lilies, convolvuli, roses, lotuses, and magnolias, is an artistic tour-de-force. From Jingdezhen, Qing dynasty, reign of Qianlong, dated 1790.

Fine ceramics continued to be made in the Yuan dynasty, with novel designs using colored glazes influenced by Western Asian imports (see page 140). Blue-and-white ware first appeared in the Yuan (see page 133), which as a whole represents a transition between the simple elegance of the Song and the more colorful porcelain of the Ming and Qing.

THE IMPERIAL KILNS: JINGDEZHEN

Of central importance in the history of Chinese porcelain is Jingdezhen in eastern China's Jiangxi province. Its development as a porcelain center was due to there being large deposits of key raw materials nearby, such as kaolin (China clay) and feldspar (China stone), as well as its position on the Yangzi River and near the Boyang Lake, which made it easy to transport finished goods by water. Ceramic production in the area started in the Han era, but it was in the early Ming that Jingdezhen became the preeminent center after the imperial kilns were established there.

The imperial kilns employed production lines, each piece passing through several hands. One craftsman would draw the first color line under the rim, another would trace the design, which a third would then paint. Artists would specialize, one in mountains and water, another in birds and animals, and so on. Embossing, engraving, and openwork carving would likewise be entrusted to separate hands. Up to seventy workmen might be involved before the pieces were ready for firing.

With the development of new techniques in the Yuan, Ming, and Qing dynasties, the order of these processes might be changed, depending on the style of the vessel being made. In the case of the blue-and-white vessels, which became popular in the last three dynasties, the blue underglaze would be added first before firing at a high temperature, whereas Qing dynasty *famille rose* vessels would be painted after a first firing at a relatively low temperature. Sometimes gilt decoration was added by firing for a third time. Another colored porcelain, *famille verte*, is noted for its dominant brilliant green enamel. Other types of Jingdezhen porcelain include the green or green-blue celadon, which originated in Zhejiang, and *wucai*, or five-color porcelain (red, yellow, green, blue, and purple). Very fine translucent vessels, such as eggshell porcelain, were shaved thin on a lathe. Sometimes large pieces were produced in parts and luted together after firing.

There were also private kilns in Jingdezhen, the products of which were more varied in quality but at times matched those of the imperial ones. The city continues to dominate ceramic production in China today and is also a major tourist attraction.

RIGHT
A *famille verte* vase decorated with scenes of rice farming and, shown here, silk production, based on the *Gengzhi tu*, a popular work illustrating aspects of agriculture. From Jingdezhen, Qing dynasty, 18th century.

AN AGE OF SPLENDOR

The Early Ming Dynasty (1368–ca. 1450)

OPPOSITE
Ming craftsmen perfected the art of *cloisonné* enamel decoration in the 15th century. This elaborately finished jar is embellished with a dragon and imperial insignia. Enameled brass, Ming dynasty, reign of Xuande (1426–1435).

BELOW
The emperor Hongwu (ruled 1368–1398), founder of the Ming dynasty, aged about 62. Ink and watercolor on paper, Ming dynasty, ca. 1390.

Zhu Yuanzhang assumed the reign title Hongwu ("Military Splendor"), and reigned for thirty years (1368–1398) from Nanjing, the first capital of the Ming dynasty. After he had driven the Yuan court from Beijing in 1369, it fled back into Mongolia; Hongwu's armies followed and in 1372 captured the Mongols' northern capital of Karakorum. This was the end of Mongol rule in China, although the Mongols remained a threat to the northern frontier. During his rule, Hongwu carried out some groundbreaking reforms that laid the foundations for the successes of the dynasty. The most impressive of these were the measures taken to restore agriculture after the devastation caused by the numerous rebellions that had marked the latter years of the Yuan. Destitute farmers were employed to repair watercourses and reservoirs, and to construct new ones. Large areas of land were repopulated with people from other areas, who were granted exemption from taxation, so that within ten years grain output increased threefold. Millions of trees were planted, including larger varieties for construction purposes, which would also provide timber for seagoing ships. In the early Ming there was a great expansion of maritime trade, and most of the transportation of goods from southern China to the north was by sea, hence the need to construct large wooden vessels. It was made compulsory for farming families to plant smaller trees, such as mulberry, persimmon, and jujube, in order to provide fruit or leaves for silkworms.

These achievements were impressive in themselves but in a way they marked a step backward from the policies of the Song and Yuan dynasties, whose revenues had come largely from commercial taxation. Agriculture had not been the main source of government income since the early Tang, but it would become so during both the Ming and Qing dynasties.

Aspects of Hongwu's policies owed something to the precedents set by the Mongols. One of these was a propensity to divide the population into categories or castes based on their professions. In theory these categories were

supposed to be permanent: thus, for example, if a boy was born into a peasant family he in turn had to become a peasant, as did all his descendants. The same applied to soldiers and craftsmen. One aim of this system was to ensure a constant supply of troops for the army and of craftsmen for the state workshops. But it depended on accurate records being maintained, which proved to be beyond the capacity of the Ming, just as had been the case in previous dynasties, and within a few decades the records no longer conformed to reality. This had a detrimental effect on the regime's tax revenues.

THE ASCENDANCY OF THE EUNUCH

Another weakness of Hongwu's reign was his distrust of the scholar elite, who had enjoyed a high status during the Song dynasty and had still found a role, albeit more restricted, under the Yuan. The first Ming emperor was a northerner and a peasant and preferred to trust people with whom he spoke a common language. That is one reason why he started a trend which in the end was to prove fatal to the dynasty: the employment of eunuchs in positions of trust.

Most of the eunuchs were themselves northerners and in spite of at first being forbidden to become literate, they soon became indispensible to the dynasty and were employed in some of the most responsible positions, including control of the Embroidered Gown Guard (Jin Yi Wei), the Ming secret police. Toward the end of the

LEFT
In 1391 the emperor Hongwu introduced the *buzi*, or embroidered badge of rank, worn on the robes of civil and military officials. This 17th-century example depicts the *qilin* (see illustration page 141), denoting a military official of the highest rank. *Buzi*, also known as "mandarin squares," were worn until the end of the imperial period in 1912.

RIGHT
Owing to its association with the Yuan dynasty, Tibetan Buddhism lacked popular support during the Ming dynasty. However, Yongle and other individual rulers were keen supporters and patronized several Tibetan temples in Beijing. This embroidered and appliqued banner was used in Tibetan Buddhist rites. Ming dynasty.

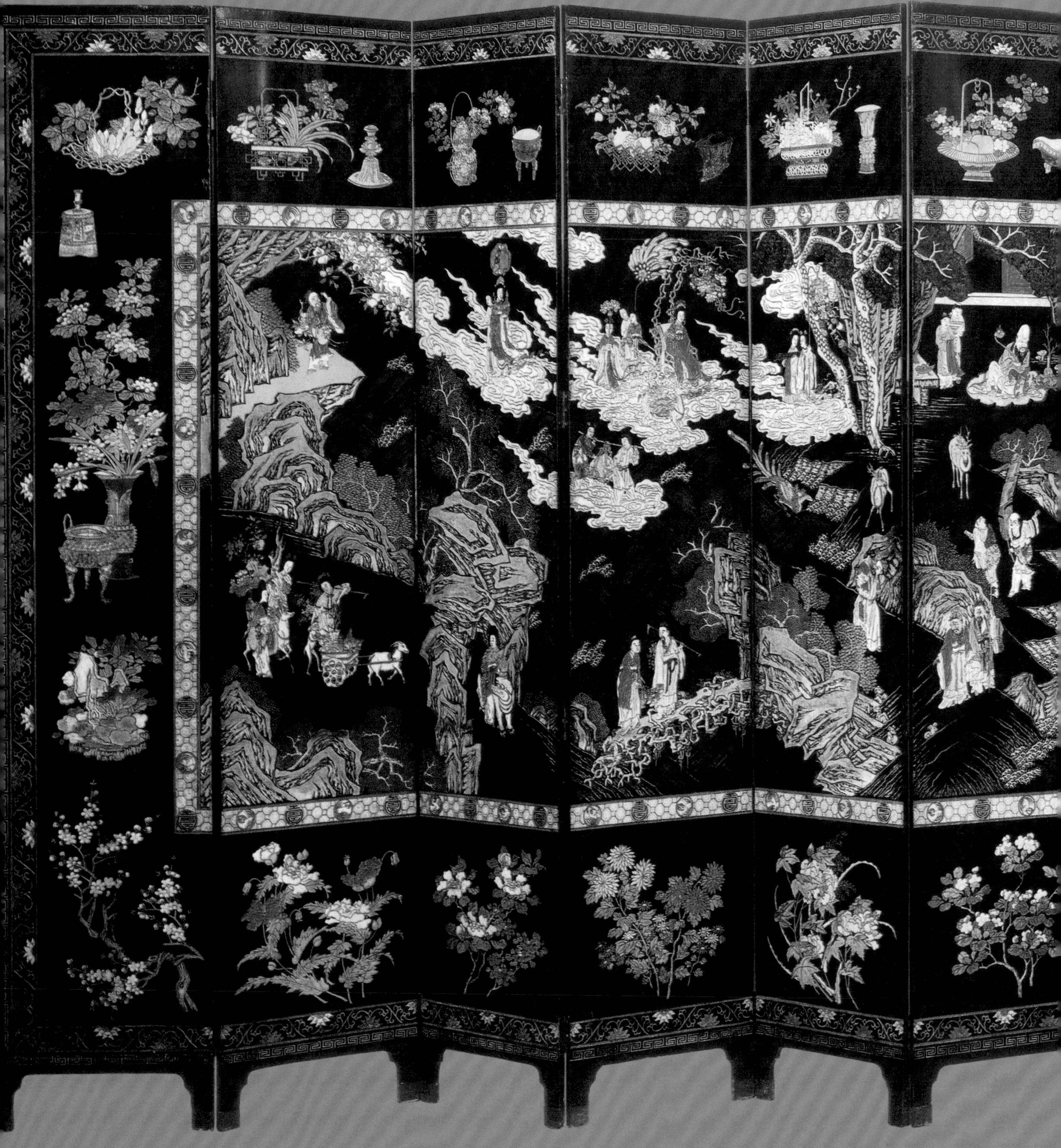

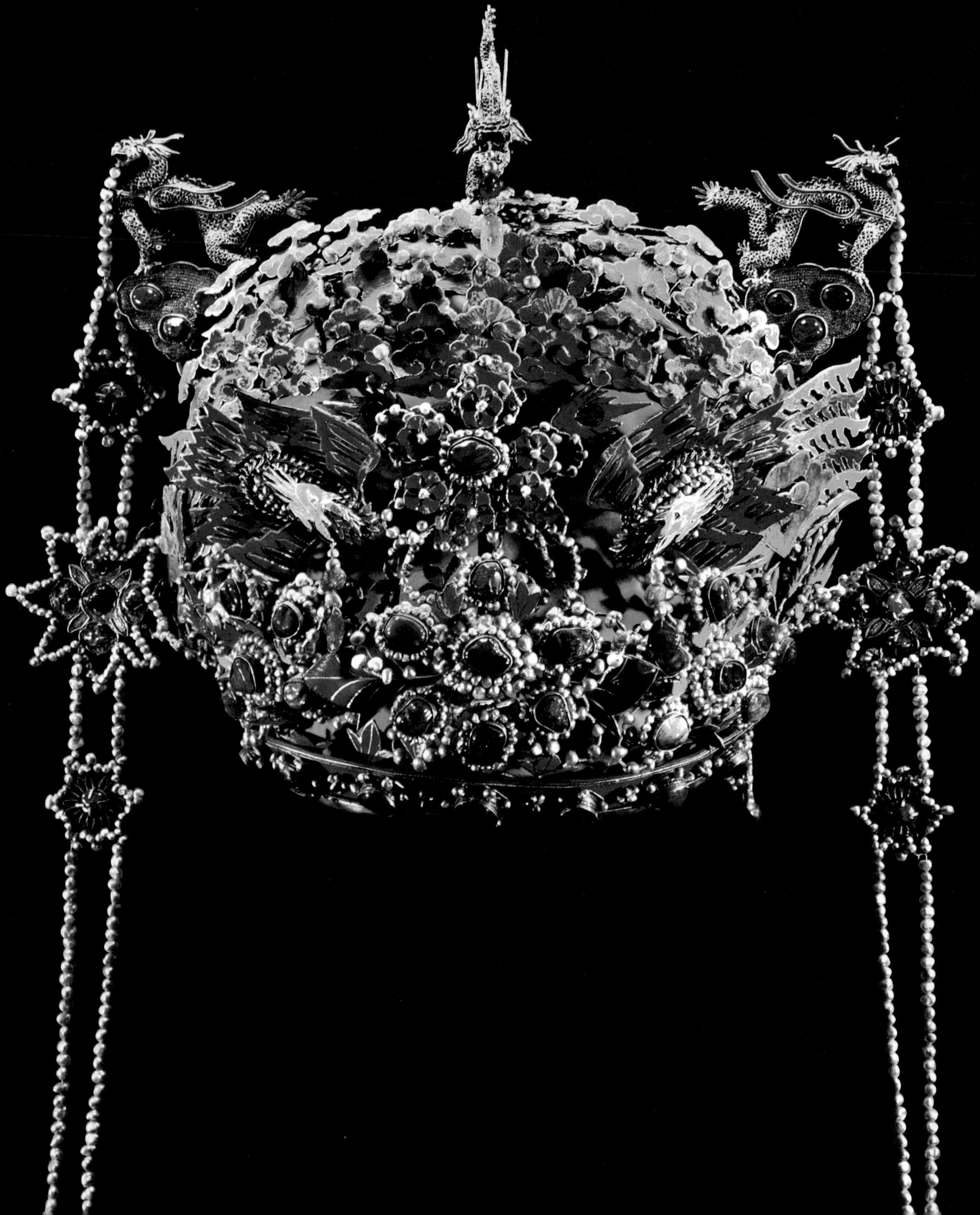

PRECEDING PAGES
This folding screen adorned the reception room of a wealthy family. The scene depicted is the birthday of Xi Wang Mu, the "Queen Mother of the West," who is receiving the peaches of eternal life from the Eight Immortals (see caption, page 156). Tinted lacquer and oil paint applied to carved laquer on wood, ca. 1625–1650.

OPPOSITE
A "phoenix crown" worn by a Ming empress on ceremonial occasions. Constructed on a base of lacquered bamboo and green silk, the crown is decorated with jade phoenixes (emblems of an empress) and gold dragons, as well as gemstone flowers. The crown bears around 150 precious gems and more than 5,000 pearls.

BELOW
Bixia Yuanjun, "Princess of the Azure Clouds," benevolent goddess of children, women, and destiny, became increasingly popular under the Ming, drawing thousands to her shrine on China's most sacred mountain, Taishan (Mount Tai) in Shandong. Painted and partly gilded wood, Ming dynasty.

dynasty the eunuchs became one of the major powers in the imperial administration, numbering as many as 70,000, sponsoring a large program of temple building, and often coming into direct conflict with the regular bureaucracy.

THE MING GREAT WALL

The Great Wall of China was first constructed by the Qin dynasty, a millennium and a half earlier, and had been added to and repaired many times since. But it was the Ming dynasty that undertook the major reconstruction of the wall that gave it the form that is familiar to most visitors today. The first repairs were undertaken by Hongwu, who had just defeated the Mongols and still viewed them as his main enemies, but they were carried forward by the third Ming emperor, Yongle (1402–1424) and his successors, taking in all about two centuries to complete. Having moved the capital north from Nanjing to Beijing, very near to the eastern section of the wall, Yongle must have been partly motivated by the need to defend his base. However, he did not confine his reconstruction to east China, but also completed the spectacular fort at the western end of the wall in Gansu province at Jiayu Pass (see page 152).

Another major work undertaken by Hongwu was the repair and expansion of the Great Mosque at Chang'an (Xi'an, see page 166). Situated near the center of the modern city and still in regular use, the mosque was founded in 742 CE during the Tang dynasty to serve the spiritual needs of the many Arab and Persian merchants who travelled to China along the Silk Road. By the Ming dynasty there was even more such trade, which the emperor wished to promote. At

first sight the Xi'an complex looks nothing like a Middle Eastern mosque. It is built entirely in a Chinese style, with buildings similar to Chinese wooden temples or palaces, separated by courtyards, with ceremonial arches, gates, stone tablets, and other Chinese features rather than domes and minarets. There are even inscriptions by such famous Chinese calligraphers as Mi Fei of the Song dynasty and Dong Qichang of the Ming.

But within the complex there are all the requisites of a mosque. The main building in the third courtyard is a prayer hall for up to 1,000 worshippers, and there is also a two-story building that serves as a minaret, and another where worshippers can perform the necessary ritual ablutions. The complete Quran is inscribed on large wooden boards, and there are many other Arabic inscriptions. Some of these features were added later but the main reconstruction was in the early Ming era. The Great Mosque remains the main place of worship for Xian's 100,000 Muslim residents.

ABOVE
The great fort of Jiayuguan (Jiayu Pass) in Gansu province was constructed in the early Ming dynasty as the first pass in the western end of the Great Wall (see page 151).

In spite of his early achievements, Hongwu became increasingly autocratic and paranoid. He even became suspicious of some who had always supported him and served him well, but who in his view had become too powerful. Often they were accused because of innocently using certain words which were interpreted as implying criticism. Hongwu staged a number of show trials, which ended in the death penalty for the unfortunate victims. One important official to suffer in this way was his old comrade-in-arms and fellow provincial Hu Weiyong, who was wrongly accused of planning a rebellion and being in league with the Japanese and Mongols. Thousands of people were dragged into the trial, which ended in the emperor abolishing the Grand Secretariat and taking direct control of the government himself.

OPPOSITE
This dish is among the earliest known polychrome carved lacquer items depicting a popular scene, in this case "the festival at Lanting Pavilion." Ming dynasty, dated 1489. (See also pages 166–168.)

PERPETUAL HAPPINESS: YONGLE

Hongwu was succeeded by the young emperor Jianwen (1398–1402). He tried to sideline the powerful royal princes, with the consequence that in 1402 his uncle Zhu Di, the prince of Yan, deposed him with the support of the other

princes. Zhu Di chose the title Yongle ("Perpetual Happiness"), and his reign (1402–1424) is remembered for a number of achievements. His power base was Beijing ("Northern Capital"), the old Yuan capital of Dadu, of which he had been governor, and in 1406 work began there on the construction of a new imperial palace, which still stands today. "The Great Within," better known as the "Forbidden City," was situated on the same site as the Yuan-dynasty palaces, but slightly to the south. Some additions and alterations to the original buildings were made during the later Ming and the Qing dynasties but the traditional north–south alignment of the main buildings was always adhered to (see pages 190–195). In 1415 Yongle decided to move the imperial capital to Beijing from the early Ming capital of Nanjing ("Southern Capital").

ABOVE
A stone sculpture depicting two officials, one military (left) and the other civil (right). The civil official is shown wearing the "mandarin square," or *buzi*, that indicates his rank (see page 146). Ming dynasty.

OPPOSITE
This pendant would have been worn by a wealthy bride and bears the auspicious symbols of the phoenix (a mythical bird unrelated to the Western phoenix) on one side and the *qilin* (mythical beast—see page 141) on the other. Gold and semiprecious stones with silk tassels, Ming dynasty.

THE VOYAGES OF ZHENG HE

Among the other achievements of the Yongle period were the remarkable voyages of the great navigator Zheng He (1371–1433). A Muslim from Yunnan, Zheng became a eunuch after Yunnan was conquered by the prince of Yan in 1382 and entered the prince's service. He went on to hold several military posts, and after his master became the emperor Yongle, Zheng was put in charge of a series of maritime expeditions (1403–1425) involving several dozen seagoing junks carrying more than 20,000 men on each voyage. The largest junks in Zheng He's fleet were over 425 ft (130 m) long and over 160 ft (50 m) wide, carried nine sails, and were the biggest and most efficient ships in the world at the time.

Zheng He's aim was to impress the rulers of the states of Southeast and South Asia by Chinese wealth and power, obtain tribute from them, and facilitate trade relations. These aims were largely achieved. Among the countries and ports Zheng He visited were Java, Sumatra, Malacca, Thailand, Sri Lanka, Calicut, Cochin, and he even voyaged across the Indian Ocean as far as Aden (Yemen) and the vicinity of Mogadishu in East Africa. In several places the Chinese intervened or negotiated between parties in local disputes.

Zheng He's expeditions were on a larger scale and more far-reaching than the pioneering Portuguese voyages nearly a century later, but they marked the greatest extent of Chinese overseas adventures and from that point on there was a decline in China's sea power. In 1411–1415, the Ming undertook improvements to the Grand Canal (see pages 80–82), which had deteriorated over the centuries, so that from then on south–north transportation switched back to the canal, cutting out most of the hazards of sea voyages. This also had the effect of ending imperial support for long distance sea exploration, so that Zheng He's voyages turned out to be unique in Chinese history.

ABOVE
Symbolizing Heaven and immortality, jade was a highly prestigious material. Only the wealthiest patrons could have afforded jade vessels such as this bowl. Not only was it immensely difficult to create delicate thin curved walls, carving a bowl from a large block of highly valuable jade also involved a great deal of wastage. Ming dynasty.

THE GREAT ENCYCLOPEDIA

Another major achievement of Yongle's reign was the compilation of the *Yongle Encyclopedia*. This enormous pioneering work was commissioned early in Yongle's reign after he had been impressed by some less ambitious works that had been presented to him by their compilers. The emperor ordered the production of a far greater work that was to embrace in a single collection the important contents of all existing books then available. It was an enormous undertaking. The emperor appointed five chief compilers and twenty assistants, and dispatched scholars all over the empire to search for material. The *Yongle Encyclopedia* was completed in five years and transcribed by expert calligraphers. It had altogether 22,937 chapters, contained in 11,095 volumes, and embraced most areas of knowledge. Unfortunately most of the copies that were commissioned have been lost, and only 800 chapters are extant, some in foreign collections.

Few of the later Ming emperors matched the ability or achievements of Hongwu and Yongle. The decline in Chinese sea power following the repairs to the Grand Canal was matched by a weakening of the Ming's active policy in the north. This policy became more and more defensive, coinciding with a more aggressive effort by the old Mongol enemy to drive the Chinese back to the plains. Much of this conflict resulted from the policy of the Ming of restricting trade with the Mongols by putting an embargo on the export of armaments and the metals from which they could be manufactured. The Mongol attacks were eventually to culminate in the capture of the Ming emperor Zhengtong at the battle of Tumu Fortress in northern Hebei in 1449. Zhengtong was eventually released by the Mongols until 1457 and resumed his reign, but the episode caused enormous damage to the prestige of Ming China.

OPPOSITE
Three of the Eight Immortals, central figures in Daoist mythology. Shown here are the flute-playing minstrel Lan Caihe and (far right) the quasihistorical Cao Guojiu, a brother of an empress, who bears his gold tablet for admission to court; the pair flank He Xiangu, the only Immortal who was definitely female, who grinds the elixir of eternal life. Ivory, late Ming dynasty.

THE TEMPLE OF HEAVEN

The Sacred Heart of the Empire

In 1420 the emperor Yongle ordered the construction of an altar and temple in Beijing where he could carry out his annual sacrifice to Heaven and Earth. A century later the emperor Jiajing (1522–1567) decided to separate these ceremonies and build another altar within the city for the sacrifice to Earth. Since then the original temple assumed the name by which it has since been known: the Temple of Heaven.

The temple is a complex of buildings to the south of the old central-southern city gate of Beijing, the Qianmen. It is set in a park which on weekends is alive with the sound of amateur opera singers and musicians practicing their art. The construction of the complex has many features that are symbolic of Heaven or Earth. For example it is surrounded by two walls: an inner and an outer wall. The outer wall has a rounded outer section representing Heaven and a shorter rectangular one representing the Earth. Within its walls the complex of ceremonial buildings is surrounded by an extensive

RIGHT
The interior of the Qi Nian Dian (Hall of Prayers for a Good Harvest), the most sacred ritual building in imperial China. The central part of the roof is supported on pillars in the form of a square, representing the seasons (see also page 161).

BELOW
The emperor would be carried in a litter up to the Qi Nian Dian over this carved marble panel; his courtiers and other attendants used the flanking steps.

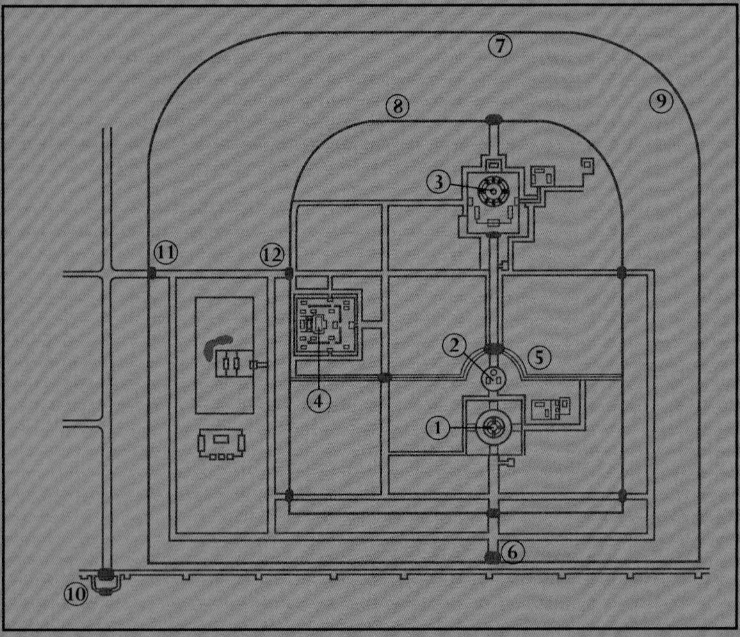

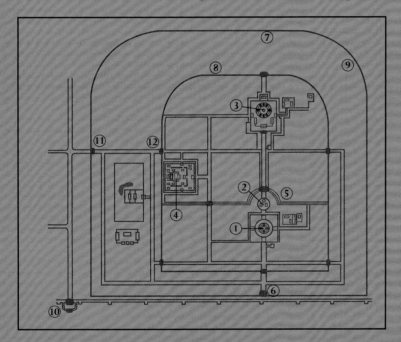

The main parts of the Temple of Heaven are: 1. Altar of Heaven, 2. Temple of the Heavenly Lord, 3. Hall of Prayers for a Good Harvest, 4. Palace of Abstinence, 5. "Echo Wall," 6. South Gate, 7. North Gate, 8. Inner Wall, 9. Outer Wall, 10. Yongdingmen Gate, 11. West Gate and 12. Gate of Western Heaven.

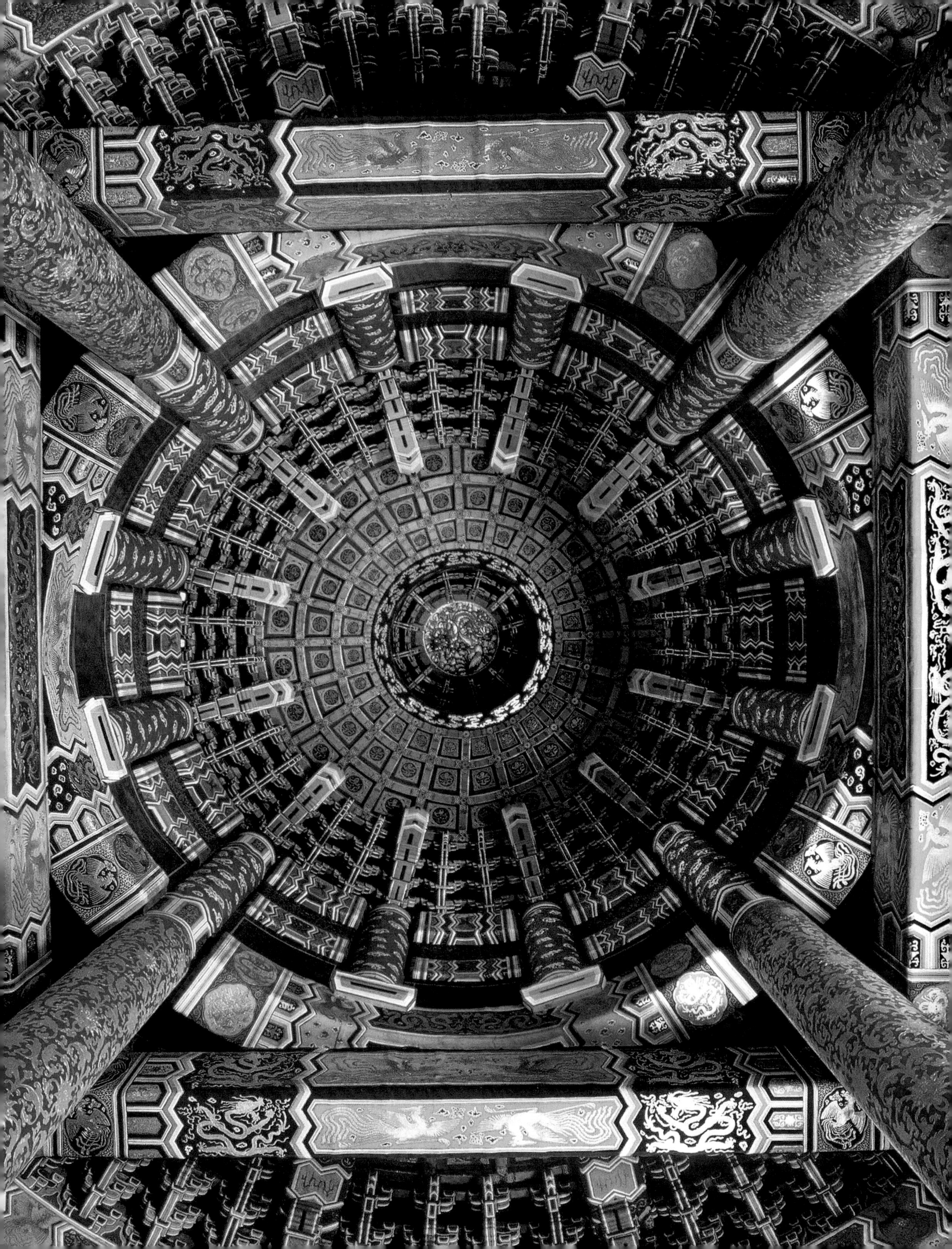

ABOVE, LEFT
Part of the sculpted stone fence surrounding the Hall of Prayers for a Good Harvest.

ABOVE, RIGHT
Recently restored, the exterior of the Hall of Prayers for a Good Harvest is a blaze of auspicious colors and motifs.

garden containing many ancient cypress and pine trees. It includes an open-air altar on a raised terrace at the southern end, and a round blue-tiled temple at the northern end, with a paved avenue linking the two. Between these two features is another smaller temple, the Temple of the Heavenly Lord, and various other buildings. These are enclosed in a round, gray wall topped with blue tiles. This wall has unusual acoustic qualities: a person whispering at the north end can be heard clearly at the south end.

THE TEMPLE OF GOOD HARVESTS

The large, round temple building at the north end is the Qi Nian Dian (Hall of Prayers for a Good Harvest) where the emperor came to pray to Heaven each year on the eighth day of the first lunar month. This temple was the most important enclosed ritual space in imperial China, since the wellbeing of the empire and people were believed to depend on the correct performance of rituals here. As a construction, it is noted not only for its roof of bright blue glazed tiles, but also for its interior construction. Basically it is a wooden framed building, like all the other palace buildings in Beijing, but because of its round construction and conical roof, the brackets above the columns are

ABOVE
The Hall of Prayers for a Good Harvest is circular in form, representing Heaven in traditional Chinese cosmology. Once the tallest building in Beijing, it stands 105 ft (32 m) high and 98 ft (30 m) in diameter. Despite its size, the structure is supported on a mere 28 wooden pillars (see page 159).

concentrated into a smaller and smaller area. Like the rest of the interior woodwork they are painted in multicolored patterns, so that the view looking upward from the floor of the temple is particularly striking. The roof is supported by three groups of columns: four inner columns—the Dragon Well Pillars—representing the four seasons, and two sets of twelve columns, an inner set representing the twelve months of the year and an outer for day and night in traditional Chinese hours (two hours each).

The altar consists of three marble terraces mounted by steps and surrounded by carved marble balustrades. The details of the steps and balustrades are in multiples of nine, which is the emperor's lucky number. After carrying out his ceremony in the Prayer Temple, the emperor would process southward toward the other ceremonial buildings and the altar. On the way he stopped off at a platform halfway along the route where a tent was erected in which he changed his ceremonial robes.

The last time these ceremonies were carried out was in the final year of the Qing dynasty. Attempts by some members of the new republican government to continue them failed, and since that time the temple has been preserved for the Chinese people as a national monument and public park.

明

A SLOW UNRAVELING

The Later Ming (ca. 1450–1644)

明 After the Yongle period the highly centralized systems instituted at the beginning of the dynasty were gradually undermined, and more freedom from the control of central government facilitated individual initiative, though it was never allowed to get entirely out of hand. During the fifteenth and particularly the sixteenth centuries the increase in the use of silver as the basic method of payment brought great benefit to trade and industry. It led to the development of the Shanxi silver firms, which brought credit within reach of the traders, as well as prosperity to the Shanxi bankers themselves, who spread their activities outside their native province. Commerce and handicraft manufacture took over from land as the most lucrative businesses, especially in the maritime provinces of the south and southeast.

However, at the beginning of the seventeenth century the Ming dynasty began to unravel. At the heart of the trouble was the increasingly bitter dispute between the eunuchs, who had the ears of successive weak emperors, and the regular scholar-officials, many of whom had been dismissed from their posts at the instigation of the eunuchs. From about 1615 onward the latter formed parties based on various academies, of which one, the Donglin Academy at Wuxi in Jiangsu, became the main center of opposition to eunuch rule. The most notorious of the eunuchs was Wei Zhongxian, who had castrated himself in order to worm his way into the imperial palace. Once there he soon had many members of Donglin executed. On the accession of the last Ming emperor in 1628, Wei was executed and Donglin rehabilitated. But by this stage the Ming were facing a far greater crisis.

BELOW
A large *cloisonné* basin decorated with a red dragon and other auspicious emblems. *Cloisonné* is a complex process involving the creation of individual compartments (*cloisons*) of different colored enamel on a metal base (in China, usually copper). From the Ming onward, the intricate *cloisonné* of Beijing was particularly famed (see also page 145). Ming dynasty, reign of Wanli (1573–1620).

THE FALL OF THE MING

In the last half century of Ming rule a combination of corruption among the court eunuchs, a huge and expensive imperial clan, and disastrous campaigns in Korea had severely drained the imperial finances. Added to this, the onset of the "Little Ice Age" of the seventeenth century had caused crops to fail, and the Ming armies could not cope with the ensuing rise in banditry across the country. In the years 1627–1628 a number of violent rebellions broke out in several parts of China. The most serious was triggered by a succession of bad harvests in the northwest, which caused widespread suffering among the peasants. There was also increasing disaffection among the garrisons in the region, many of the soldiers having been discharged to save the government money.

Soon most of the provinces of northern China were affected and eventually the separate groups of rebels were organized under the leadership of a former shepherd named Li Zicheng. He attempted to organize a rival regime in Henan province, and later moved to Chang'an, from where he prepared to march on Beijing. In April 1644 he occupied the capital and the last Ming emperor, Chongzhen (1628–1644), committed suicide on a hill overlooking the Forbidden City.

At the same time as Li Zicheng's revolt a second rebellion had broken out in Hubei province, north of the Yangzi River, and by 1644 had taken over Sichuan in the west. The leader of this uprising, Zhang Xianzhong, became increasingly tyrannical and brutal, and his activities further weakened the Ming grip on power. However, it was another threat that was to bring about

RIGHT
With the exception of the fanatically Daoist Jiajing (1522–1567), the Ming emperors were devout Buddhists. Tibetan styles influenced Buddhist sculpture at this time, but the soft rendering of the cloth and lack of inlaid gemstones on this figure of the meditating Buddha are distinctly Chinese. Gilt bronze, Ming dynasty, 16th century.

the final downfall of the dynasty. This came from a Tungusic people descended from the Jurchens who had ruled the north of China as the Jin dynasty in the twelfth and thirteenth centuries (see page 109) and are better known in history as the Manchus.

ARTS OF THE MING

Ming painting continued the trends introduced in the Song and Yuan periods, particularly *literati* paintings. During the last decades of the Ming dynasty, the painter Dong Qichang (1555–1636) came to prominence and his landscapes were highly prized (see page 167). His *Eight Autumn Scenes* are often reproduced in works on Chinese painting. Dong was a high official and a scholarly man of many talents and his work is thought of as more austere than emotional. At the same time he is adventurous in the way he treats landscape and sometimes sacrifices reality for artistic effect. He believed that painters should be disinterested amateurs, which is what, in theory any rate, the *literati* painters mostly were. Dong had a profound influence on artistic developments and schools of thought under the Ming and Qing dynasties. He was also a master calligrapher, upon whose style even the Qing emperor Qianlong modeled his own calligraphy.

ABOVE
By the Ming period imperial goldsmiths had become highly skilled at creating intricate filigree items such as these fittings for a headdress. Gold and precious stones, Ming dynasty, ca. 1600.

RIGHT
Portable handwarmers (*shoulu*) of copper or copper alloy reached a peak of craftsmanship in the late Ming, when they were popular status symbols for men and women alike. The heat from charcoal inside the vessel rose through its openwork lid. Beaten and pierced copper, Ming dynasty, 16th century.

ABOVE
A pavilion in the gardens of the Great Mosque (Daqingzhen Si) of Xi'an, which was restored by the Ming emperor Hongwu for the use of Muslim traders and others (see page 151). The mosque incorporates inscriptions by non-Muslims such as Dong Qichang (see opposite and page 164).

OPPOSITE
Water Buffalo, from an album entitled *Carnations* by Dong Qichang (1555–1636; see page 164), whose unconventional and unsentimental landscapes influenced many later artists. Colored ink on paper.

In complete contrast Xu Wei (1521–1593), a slightly earlier contemporary of Dong's, was an extreme individualist, both in this life and his work. He gave up his job in officialdom and devoted himself to a life of pleasure. He never had much money, but his paintings were much sought after following his death and inspired the work of the individualist artists of the Qing and the twentieth century. Xu avoided the formalism of classical Chinese landscapes and broke nature down to depict such things as torn leaves on banana trees and misshapen jagged rocks, conveyed with a few violent brush strokes.

LACQUER AND PORCELAIN

Some of the best examples of lacquerwork, both large and small, were produced in the Ming period. Chinese lacquer is a varnish made from the sap of the lacquer tree which grows in most of the provinces of western and southern China from Shanxi down to Yunnan. It is applied to a core medium, such as wood or plaster, in many thin layers and then allowed to harden before a final layer is applied. The result is a hard, smooth finish impervious to air, water, acid, or alkali. In its natural state it is a rich brown, but it is usually colored either red or black.

戴嵩

The city of Fuzhou specialized in a method called "bodiless lacquer." Layers of silk or linen were bound to the original body of clay, plaster, or wood, using lacquer as a glue. After sufficient layers had been applied, the vessel was left to dry, after which the original wood or plaster body was removed. The result was a light, resilient object on to which further layers of lacquer could be added and into which patterns could be carved.

Porcelain built on the technical advances of the Yuan, and multicolored vessels of all kinds were produced in great quantities at the imperial kilns of Jingdezhen (see pages 142–143). *Cloisonné*, or *Jingtai lan* had been introduced during the Yuan but reached a new peak of perfection in the mid-fifteenth century (see pages 145 and 162). Fuzhou lacquer, Beijing *cloisonné*, and Jingdezhen porcelain have been called the "Three Treasures" of Chinese arts and crafts.

AESTHETIC RETREAT: GARDENS

Chinese gardens were of several types: imperial gardens, which were large and spacious; temple gardens, attached to Buddhist monasteries or Daoist temples; and private gardens, intended for the enjoyment of families and their friends. Of these, the private gardens reached the height of their development in the Ming dynasty, particularly in southeast China in such places as Suzhou, Hangzhou, and Yangzhou. The Suzhou gardens are the most famous today. In their heyday they were owned by members of the *literati* and were not so much

LEFT
The technique of carving lacquer with a pictorial scene was perfected under the Ming, and items such as this box were often imperial commissions. The central scene depicts Tang-dynasty founder Li Yuan winning his wife's hand by shooting an arrow into the eye of a painted peacock. Late Ming or early Qing, 17th century.

RIGHT
Ming furniture has survived in quantity, perhaps because of its strong international aesthetic appeal. The first chairs in China, introduced ca. 1000 by nomads, were folding ones. After rigid chairs became common, folding ones continued to be made for outdoor use. Wood with iron fittings, silver inlay, and fabric seat, ca. 1600.

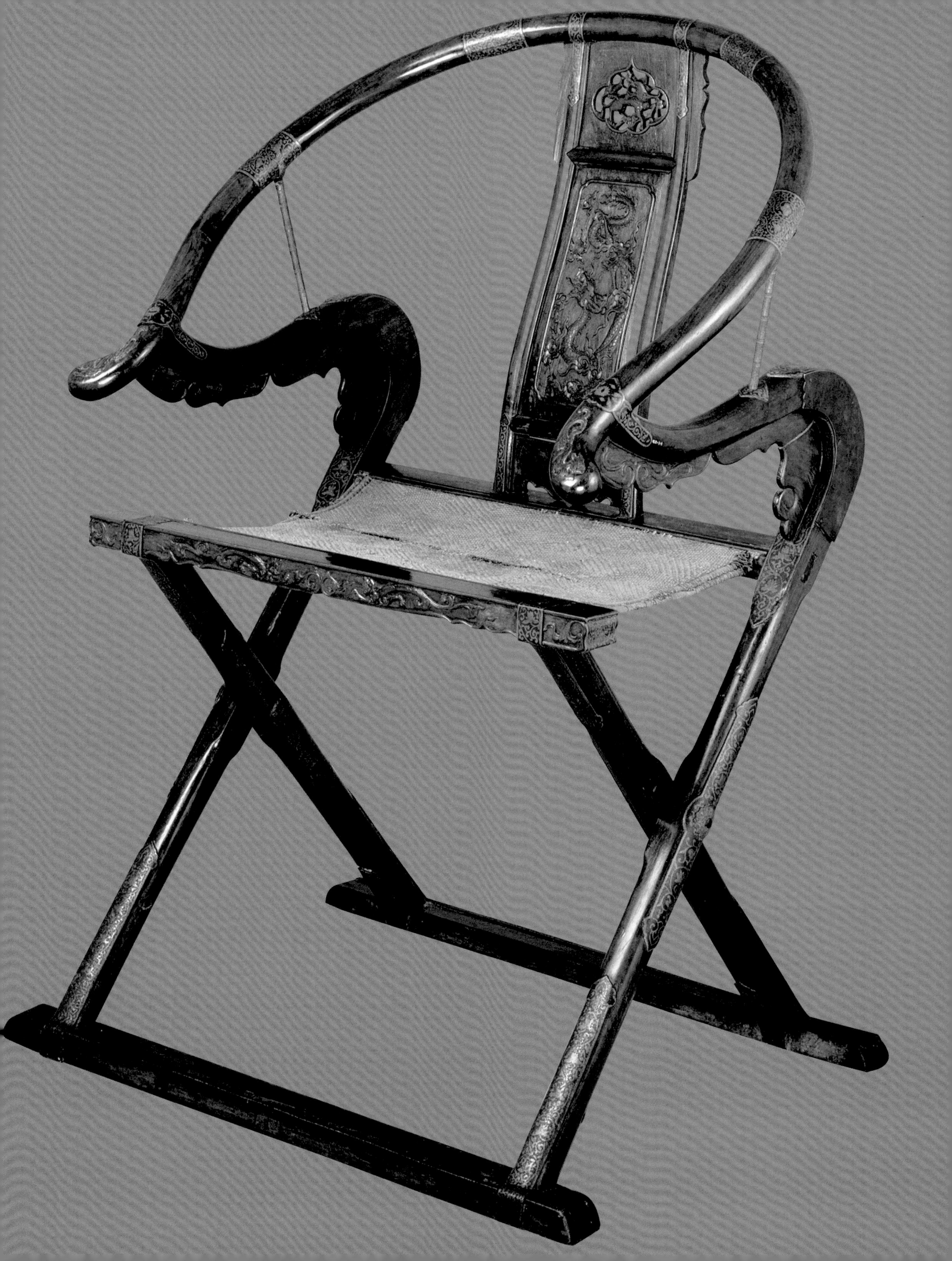

cultivated open spaces, as in the West, but settings for buildings, both residential and purely decorative, such as pavilions and shelters. The gardens were designed to be viewed from these buildings, and in addition to trees and flowers they usually had water features, ranging from ponds to ornamental rocks.

Even when gardens were not large they nevertheless created the illusion of being immersed in an extensive landscape. The rocks used in garden design were often dragged from the bottom of a large lake or a river where they had been eroded into unusual shapes. Sometimes the gardens were separated by buildings into two or three sections, or might incorporate a small island reached by a narrow bridge.

THE AGE OF THE NOVEL

Four of China's great works of fiction were written during the Ming dynasty. *The Romance of the Three Kingdoms* by Luo Guanzhong (ca. 1333–1400), the *Water Margin* by Shi Naiyan (possibly a pseudonym used by Luo Ganzhong), *Journey to the West* by Wu Cheng'en (ca. 1500–ca. 1582), and *The Plum in the Golden Vase* (or *The Golden Lotus*), which was printed anonymously in 1610. The first three are essentially adventure novels inspired by historical events, but the last is a portrait of late Ming society, with all its greed and corruption—the first long novel dealing with contemporary life in Chinese literary history. The novel's detailed descriptions of the hero's sexual activities led to its being banned for

RIGHT
The best preserved of Suzhou's gardens is the Liuyuan ("Lingering Garden"), established in 1583 by court official Xu Taishi. It is one of China's four most famous gardens, along with the Summer Palace Garden (Beijing), the Mountain Summer Resort (Chengde), and the Humble Administrator's Garden (also Suzhou).

ABOVE
The Stele Pavilion with one of its colossal ornamental columns on the "spirit way" at Shisanling, the site of the tombs of 13 Ming emperors from Yongle to the very last, Chongzhen, who committed suicide in 1644.

most of the following Qing dynasty, but it was still read widely. The author used a pseudonym and his identity remains a mystery.

Other widely read figures of the later Ming were Feng Menglong (1574–1646) and the philosopher Li Zhi (1527–1602). Feng was a prolific writer of stories based on contemporary life, many concerned with the tragedies of women trapped in slavery and prostitution. Li Zhi fiercely attacked the Song Neoconfucian Zhu Xi and advocated the freedom of the individual and equality of the sexes. This was going too far for the time; and Li Zhi was accused of "corrupting minds" and put to death.

TOMBS OF THE MING

Situated about 30 miles (50 km) northwest of Beijing is the area known as the Thirteen Tombs (Shisanling), the burial place of thirteen Ming emperors. The site was chosen by

the emperor Yongle for its geomantic properties. The tombs are distributed on a south-facing arc in a natural amphitheater of hills. They are surrounded by a wall four and a half miles (7 km) long and approached from the south by a road (the so-called *shen dao* or "spirit way") that first passes though an elaborate gate, the Great Red Gate, and eventually ends in front of the buildings of Changling, Yongle's tomb.

The burial places of the emperors are in large grave mounds behind ceremonial buildings. The latter are built on stone platforms, on the model of the main buildings of the Forbidden City in Beijing, with red walls topped by brightly colored wooden brackets supporting yellow tiled roofs. The backdrop of high wooded hills creates an impressive setting for these splendid edifices. Only three of the tombs have been partially excavated. Of these only two, Changling and Dingling, the tomb of the emperor Wanli (Shenzhong; 1573–1620), has been opened to the public with many of its contents exhibited.

ABOVE AND OPPOSITE, RIGHT
Flanking the "spirit way" leading to the Ming tombs are 24 representations of animals, including these elephants and camels, and 12 statues of civil and military officials. The latter (opposite page, right) are depicted in the ceremonial garments that would have been worn in the presence of the emperor.

七

CHAPTER SEVEN

IMPERIAL ZENITH AND DECLINE

1644 – 1911

THE QING

康熙

THE DRAGON IN THE EAST

The Age of Kangxi

OPPOSITE
A detail of a dragon from a yellow formal court robe (*chaofu*) belonging to the Qing emperor Kangxi (his grandson Qianlong wears a similar robe on page 199). Patterned silk gauze with areas of brocaded metal thread, reign of Kangxi (1661–1722).

BELOW
An anonymous court artist portrayed the youthful Kangxi in scholarly pose, wearing informal dress and holding a brush. Hanging scroll, ink and color on silk, reign of Kangxi.

The Manchus who occupied China in 1644 had grown in power over the preceding half century. By 1616 their various tribal groups had been united by force by the tribal chief Nurhaci (1559–1626), who renounced his people's nominal fealty to China and declared himself "Khan of Great Jin" in reference to his ancestors, the Jurchen, who had once ruled northern China as the Jin dynasty (see page 109). Nurhaci organized the whole Manchu population on a war footing, under eight commands, the so-called Eight Banners. This was not only a military organization, but also an administrative unit, such that every Manchu family would be assigned to a particular Banner in perpetuity. The Banners were denoted by the colors of their flags, four of them plain and four with borders.

In this way the Manchus organized a powerful military force, which turned out to be a match both for the Ming armies and for Li Zicheng's rebels who had occupied Beijing in April 1644. Shortly afterward the Manchu armies entered China from Manchuria through the pass in the Great Wall at Shanhaiguan ("Pass Between Mountain and Ocean"). According to popular legend, the Ming general Wu Sangui (1612–1678), who was defending the pass, let the invaders through because one of Li Zicheng's commanders had seized Wu's concubine and he wanted to use the Manchus to take revenge on Li. But perhaps a more likely reason for Wu Sangui's treachery was that he wished to restore order following the suicide of the last Ming emperor, Chongzheng, in the face of Li Zicheng's rebellion (see page 163). Indeed, the alliance with the Manchus was made in the name of avenging Chongzheng's death.

The combined armies of the Manchus and Wu Sangui defeated Li Zhicheng and the Manchus occupied Beijing in May 1644. A few days later, the five-year-old Manchu ruler Shunzhi was declared emperor of a new dynasty, the Qing ("Pure"), which was to turn out to be China's last. Wu Sangui was rewarded with the governorship of a large area in southwest China. He later rebelled against the Manchus—he

BELOW
A small reliquary in the form of a *chörten* or Tibetan stupa. It exemplifies the Sino-Tibetan styles of Buddhist art that evolved under the Qing, whose rulers were adherents of Tibetan Buddhism. Gilded metal and silver inlaid with ruby, turquoise, and lapis lazuli. Qing dynasty, reign of Qianlong (1735–1796).

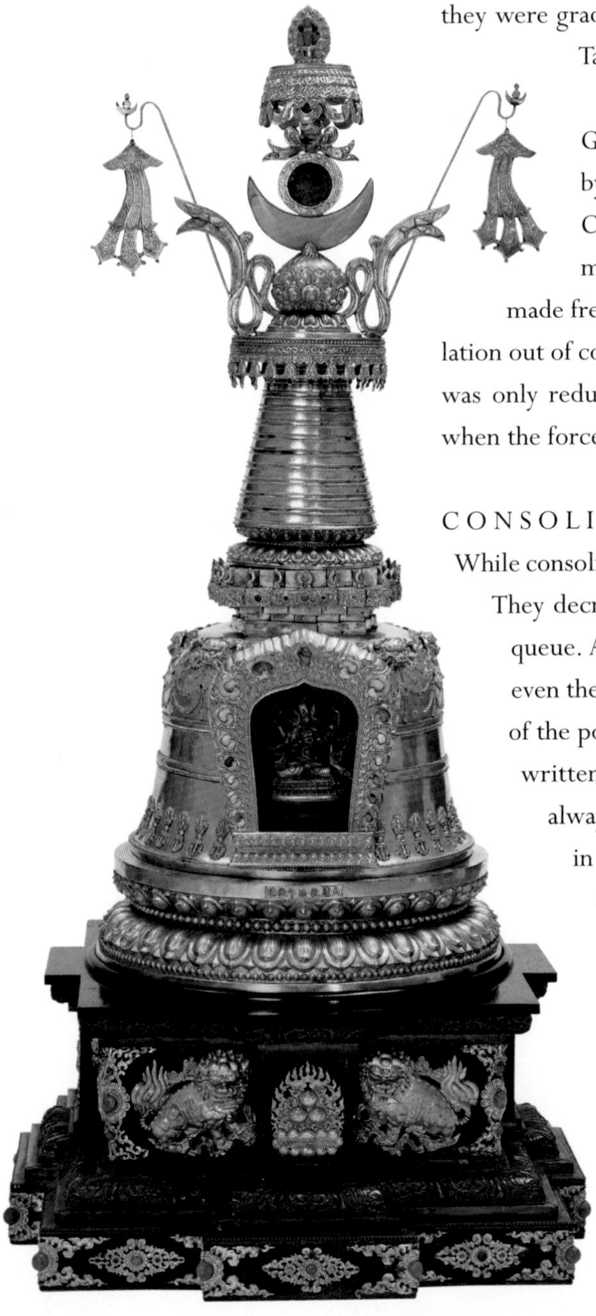

is popularly regarded as a traitor to both the Ming and Qing dynasties—but after his death in 1678 the revolt was quickly defeated.

Because of Shunzhi's age one of his uncles, Dorgun, acted as regent and it was he who was chiefly responsible for leading the conquest of the rest of mainland China. Li Zicheng was killed soon after his defeat by some local landlord militia. Zhang Xianzhong, the leader of the rebellion in Sichuan, was killed in 1647. Thereafter, military opposition to the Manchus was led by a series of officials who remained loyal to the Ming, and a succession of Ming pretenders held sway over decreasing territories, but they were gradually driven farther south and west and finally all of China apart from Taiwan was occupied by the new rulers.

An important figure in the anti-Manchu movement in the south was Guoxingye (1624–1662), a military adventurer and pirate called Coxinga by the Europeans. For several decades he raided the southeast coast of China and in 1661, after the Qing had forced him to retreat from the mainland, he defeated the Dutch occupiers of Taiwan and from there made frequent raids on China's coastal ports. The Qing cleared the entire population out of coastal territories in an extreme measure to deal with the menace, which was only reduced after Coxinga's death. His descendants ruled Taiwan until 1682, when the forces of the Kangxi emperor finally occupied the island.

CONSOLIDATION AND ASSIMILATION

While consolidating their power, the Manchus instituted a policy of harsh oppression. They decreed that all Chinese males should braid their hair together in a single queue. Any man failing to do so would be in danger of losing his head. Where even the slightest sign of rebellion was detected they instigated a mass slaughter of the population, as happened in 1645 at Yangzhou on the lower Yangzi River; a written account of the ten-day massacre survives. However, while the Manchus always remained sensitive to any hint of disaffection, they soon realized that in order to govern China they needed to win at least the tacit acceptance of their rule by the Chinese people, so such extreme measures were seldom repeated. All the same, anti-Manchu secret societies continued to exist in some areas.

Although the Qing dynasty had concentrated at the outset on crushing all military opposition, its leaders knew that to establish a new dynasty on a more permanent basis they had to restore the systems

LEFT
Ceremonial Manchu armor of the emperor Kangxi. The garment is made of cotton lined with silk and decorated with clouds and dragon motifs. Blue-black cotton with embroidery, gilt bronze bosses, and epaulettes partly gilt and inlaid with semiprecious stones. Qing dynasty, reign of Kangxi, late 17th century.

PRECEDING PAGES
Kangxi visits the Jianghan plain in 1699, during one of his six grand tours of inspection of the Yangzi region. The imperial troops march through the town gates while the townspeople look on. After a painting by Jiao Bingzhen (1689–1726), one of the first Chinese painters to adopt Western influences, for example in his use of shading; ink and color on silk-backed paper, Qing dynasty.

of government that had been successful hitherto. Thus, as early as 1646, during the minority of the first Qing emperor, Shunzhi (ruled 1644–1661), the traditional civil service examinations were restored in order to ensure a continuity of young recruits to the bureaucracy. This remained the Manchus' policy throughout their rule. Many former Ming officials and scholars who were reluctant to bow to their wishes retired to their family homes, but younger men had no alternative but to serve the Qing, just as their fathers had served the Ming.

The Qing rulers also adhered to the Confucian concept of government, especially the Neoconfucian ideas of the Song philosopher Zhu Xi (see page 120), stressing as they did the importance of loyalty to authority. Eminent Confucian scholars were employed to train the royal princes, and the emperors carried out the annual ceremonies at the Temple of Heaven (see pages 158–161) and elsewhere as former Chinese rulers had. From the top down, the Manchus sought to appear as the most devoted followers of Chinese culture.

The Manchu rulers have been described as enlightened despots and to a large extent this reputation is deserved. By adopting a policy of ruling China by Chinese methods they fostered social stability and, as far as possible, friendly relations with their neighbors. As a result the economy was able to grow and opposition to Qing rule decreased, although it never entirely disappeared. In the eighteenth century pro-Ming and other rebellions continued to erupt in Anhui, Sichuan, and elsewhere, but up to the nineteenth century, when the empire was in serious decline, such revolts were not a great threat to the dynasty.

A FAR-FLUNG EMPIRE

Shunzhi was an enthusiastic young man who tried to institute a number of reforms, but during his reign real power was exercised by such royal princes as Dorgon and Aubai (Oboi). As he grew up, Shunzhi became more and more attracted to Buddhism and even thought of abdicating the throne to become a monk. But after his early death at the age of twenty-three, a trio of able emperors came to power in succession and ruled China until the end of the eighteenth century. The first of these succeeded as an eight-year-old boy and assumed the reign title of Kangxi. His reign (1662–1722) was the longest in Chinese history, and he was also one of the most exceptionally competent emperors.

As had happened with his father, Kangxi had initially ruled through regents. When he eventually took over the reins of full power in 1669, aged fifteen, Kangxi was soon faced with a rebellion by three regional governors, led by Wu Sangui. He defeated this in 1681, and the following year Qing armies overthrew the last bastion of anti-Qing resistance in Taiwan. In 1689 Kangxi agreed a treaty with Russia that gave China the Amur valley and fixed a border between the two expanding empires.

The Qing also attempted to win over the Tibetans and the other peoples of Central Asia, with whom the Manchu historically shared nomadic traditions. To accomplish this they had to resist the ambitions of a powerful ruler called Galdan, whose territory covered a great part of the region in the late seventeenth century. Galdan was finally defeated in 1696 by Kangxi's armies and Chinese influence across the region was restored. Indeed, Tibet occupied a special position in the Qing world-view. The Qing

ABOVE
A detail of one of a series of scrolls depicting celebrations for the 60th birthday of Kangxi in 1714. This copy was commissioned in the late 18th century under Kangxi's grandson, Qianlong. Handscroll, color on silk, Qing dynasty.

ABOVE
The Ancestral Graves of the Fei Family, by Shi Tao (or Tao Ji, 1642–1707). Shi Tao was one of the so-called "individualist" painters of the early Qing, who revitalized landscape and other genres by moving away from the stricter styles of the preceding dynasty.

espoused the Tibetan form of Buddhism, and in 1652, under Kangxi's predecessor, the "Great Fifth" Dalai Lama, Ngawang Lobsang Gyatso (1612–1682) had been invited on a state visit to Beijing, where he was given an impressive welcome. Dalai Lamas were treated thereafter as unofficial chaplains to the imperial throne. In the extensive grounds of the retreat built for Kangxi at Chengde, in the hills far to the northeast of Beijing, he erected palaces in the style of the great ceremonial buildings in Lhasa, the Tibetan capital (see page 204). Partly because visitors from Tibet and Central Asia often fell victim to illness in the unfamiliar environment of Beijing city, it was here that the emperor and his court spent the summer months and where Kangxi received foreign ambassadors. Migrating in response to the seasons was part of the traditional way of life of the Manchu and other peoples of the great Asian grasslands.

Yongzheng, Kangxi's successor, gave his own palace in Beijing, the Yonghe Gong, over to the Tibetan Buddhists to become a center for their worship and study in the city. Under Qianlong, who followed Yongzheng and was the third of the able emperors, Tibet became a protectorate in 1751.

Kangxi also made six tours of inspection to the increasingly prosperous Yangzi region during his long reign (see pages 180–182). He died at the age of sixty-eight after sixty-one years on the throne and was succeeded by his fourth son, Yongzheng (ruled 1722–1735). There is some controversy over whether Yongzheng was Kangxi's first choice, since primogeniture was not the Qing dynasty's favored principle of

succession and while the outgoing emperor usually expressed a first choice, on his death there was often a bitter struggle for the throne. Nevertheless, Yongzheng was an able administrator, who built on his father's achievements, continuing and even strengthening Kangxi's taxation policies. Yongzheng only reigned for seventeen years and died suddenly while at the height of his powers.

ARTS OF THE EARLY QING

In addition to the continuation of the classical tradition of painting by some excellent artists, the new dynasty also saw a new spirit of individualism that led to a reaction against the scholasticism of the Ming. Of the individualist artists, the early Qing painter Zhu Da (ca. 1626–ca. 1705), otherwise known as Bada Shanren, was one of the most famous. A member of the old Ming royal family (Zhu was the Ming family name), Zhu Da became involved in the troubles at the end of the dynasty and decided to become a monk, but soon renounced the calling and thereafter led an eccentric and bohemian life blighted by a succession of mental breakdowns. He mostly painted birds, animals, fish, and other natural subjects, giving his subjects a quite individual personality, often with a touch of humor. His paintings were popular during his lifetime and have remained so ever since.

Shi Tao, or Daoji (1642–1707), born Zhu Ruoji, was likewise an individualist painter and a scion of the former royal family. His father had been involved in the struggle to

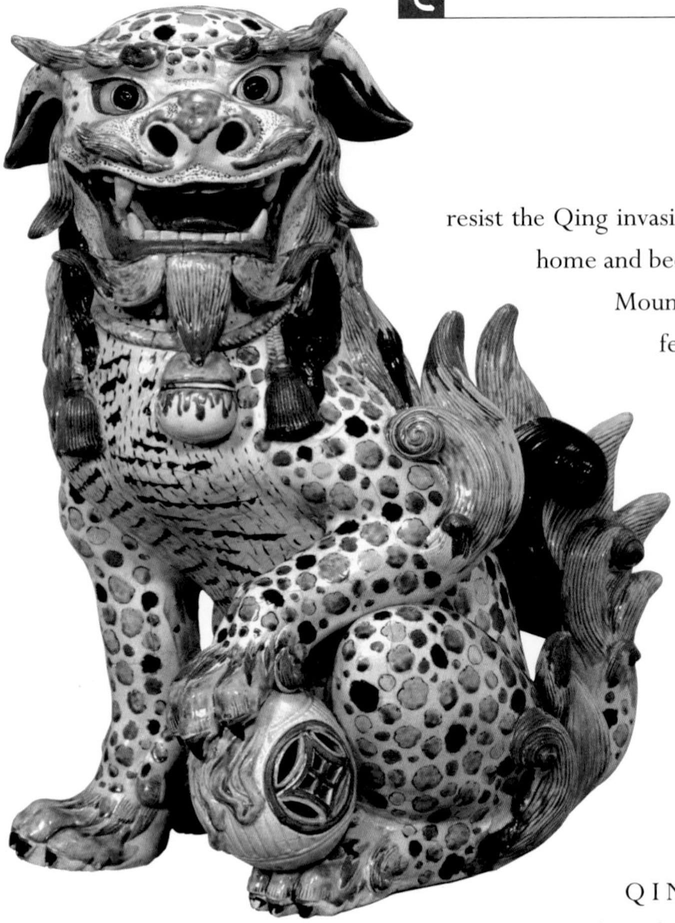

resist the Qing invasion and was captured and executed, forcing Shi Tao to leave home and become a monk. After travelling widely in the south, he visited Mount Huang in Anhui province, where he stayed for six years. He fell in love with the mountain scenery and his most successful work was done there (see pages 184–185).

Shi Tao was very versatile and also famed not just for his painting but for calligraphy, poetry, and landscape gardening. He particularly admired Ni Zan of the Yuan but he expressed the ethos of his age when he wrote the following: "The beards and eyebrows of the old masters cannot grow on my face; the lungs and bowels [thoughts and feelings] of the old masters cannot be transferred into my stomach [mind]." This was quite a revolutionary statement for the time in a country in which reverence for the past had been a cornerstone of orthodoxy.

QING CERAMICS

The volume of ceramic production increased during the Qing. Blue-and-white pottery was the most common type, but all the technical innovations introduced under the Yuan and Ming were continued in the Qing, and skilled imitations of *Ru* and other earlier wares were also produced at the imperial kilns of Jingdezhen. It was during this period that this great porcelain center (see pages 142–143) reached its zenith, with both the imperial and privately owned kilns producing wares such as *famille verte*, *famille rose*, "oxblood," and "peach bloom" for the court, for general sale, and for export, especially to an increasingly appreciative Western market.

In addition to the ceramics produced by the imperial kilns, a number of other wares were popular. Yixing, named for the city of the same name in Jiangsu province, where production was centered, is the name given to three basic types of unglazed stoneware: "purple clay" (*zisha* or *zini*, actually a purplish brown), "cinnabar clay" (*zhuni*; its red color was in fact due to iron ore), and "strengthened clay" (*duanni*), which combined the other two types with aditional minerals to make a wider range of shades, including green and black. Yixing was always unglazed: its porosity was said to enhance the flavor of tea and it was used, unsurprisingly, to make teapots in large quantities, as well as objects for scholars' desks. By the early Qing period much Yixing ware was being exported to Europe.

ABOVE
A "lion-dog" or "dog of Fo" (Buddha). Pairs of these hybrid guardian creatures, sculpted in stone or bronze, flanked the entrances to Buddhist temples, and miniature ones such as this became popular during the Qing to ward off ill fortune in homes and other buildings. Porcelain, Qing dynasty, 17th century.

OPPOSITE
The badges of rank introduced by the Ming (see page 146) continued in use, with small modifications, under the Qing. This one displays a crane, the insignia of a civil official of the first rank. Satin and silk with embroidery, feathers, and gold thread, Qing dynasty, reign of Kangxi.

Also popular during the Qing was Dehua ware, or *blanc de Chine* ("China white"). This porcelain has been manufactured in the county of Dehua, Fujian province, from the Ming dynasty until the present day. Exported to the West under the Qing in the seventeenth and eighteenth centuries, it was dubbed *blanc de Chine* on account of its crisp whiteness. It was commonly used to make statues of Buddhist divinities and other devotional objects, such as candlesticks and incense burners, perhaps because the color white has reverential associations in China (it is the color of mourning and filial piety, for example). Strictly speaking, the term "Dehua ware" refers only to the finest examples, made in Dehua itself; otherwise the more general term "Fujian ware" is used for lesser *blanc de Chine* objects such as household crockery and other artifacts.

ARTS OF THE BUDDHA

As followers of Tibetan Buddhism, the Qing emperors were revered (and portrayed) as incarnations of Manjushri, the *bodhisattva* of wisdom. The distinctive Sino-Tibetan style of Buddhist art that had developed under the Yuan continued to evolve under the Qing. Among the first acts of the new dynasty was the construction of a Tibetan-style stupa in Beihai Park in Beijing, and other quasi-Tibetan buildings were erected at the imperial retreat at Chengde (see pages 184 and 204). Tibetan styles were also used for a range of devotional artifacts, such as mandalas and reliquaries (see illustration, right, and page 178).

Notwithstanding their private devotion to Tibetan Buddhism, Kangxi and his successors were keen to be seen as assiduous students of traditional Chinese culture and practiced calligraphy and wrote poetry with even more devotion than many of their Chinese predecessors. They commissioned the dynastic history of the Ming; the biggest dictionary of Chinese yet compiled, with 45,000 entries; and the publication of a compendious collection of books in Chinese in four parts, which in scale surpassed even the *Yongle Encyclopedia* (see page 156). However, they were careful to exclude from these works any words or ideas that were critical of themselves. Lacking outlets for independent thought, the educated elite turned to classical Chinese scholarship, pursuing what was termed *kaozheng xue*, or "research based on evidence," a rigorous historical examination of classical fields of study (see pages 206–207).

OPPOSITE
Mandalas—representations of the Buddhist cosmos—feature strongly in Tibetan Buddhism and may come in many forms. This exquisite three-dimensional example opens to reveal an esoteric manifestation of the Buddha surrounded by female deities. It is another example of the Sino-Tibetan styles that evolved under the Qing (see also page 178). Gilded bronze, Qing dynasty, 17th or 18th century.

THE FORBIDDEN CITY

The Great Within

When the Yongle emperor of the Ming (ruled 1403–1424) embarked on the construction of a palace in his new capital, Beijing, he had plenty of precedents upon which to draw. The general plan of the imperial palace had been established by the Sui and Tang, and Yongle had already completed the first Ming palace, built by his father Hongwu in Nanjing. It was this palace (destroyed by the Qing in 1644) upon which was based the design of what was to be China's last seat of imperial government. Modified and expanded under the Qing, it was named the Great Within, and is better known today as the Forbidden City.

BUILDING FOR THE EMPEROR

Chinese domestic buildings were constructed from whatever local material suited the builders best; in the northern plains this was predominantly adobe, but in the south and in hilly areas stone was frequently used. However, imperial palaces, other official buildings, temple halls, and larger houses were almost invariably of wood, which is why so

RIGHT
A Scene Described in the Qianlong Emperor's Poem Bird's-Eye View of the Capital, by the court artist Xu Yang. It depicts the snow-covered Forbidden City looking north. Qing dynasty, reign of Qianlong, 1747.

BELOW
This view of the Forbidden City, looking south toward the skyline of modern Beijing, clearly shows the imperial palace's central north–south axis, on which stand the palace's principal structures, with subsidiary buildings on either side.

ABOVE
A gilt bronze altar next to the Palace of Heavenly Purity in the Inner Palace, the administrative heart of the empire. It was the residence of the first Qing emperors, but out of respect for Kangxi, who lived here for sixty years, those from Yongzheng onward occupied a smaller palace to the west.

PRECEDING PAGES
Hall of Supreme Harmony Square in the Outer Court, the ceremonial heart of the empire. The north side is dominated (right) by the hall for which it is named, the seat of the imperial throne.

few early buildings have survived—the great majority were burnt down by the various rebel armies that overthrew their occupants. On the other hand, if not deliberately destroyed, timber buildings can be remarkably durable—some non-imperial buildings, such as monastic halls, have survived for many centuries and in rare cases over a millennium in spite of storms, earthquakes, and other natural hazards. This is due to the ability of wooden structures to expand and contract in response to the climate, and also to the clever geometry of their columns, rafters, and brackets, as seen in the Forbidden City.

From the Song dynasty onward the main buildings of imperial palaces were constructed on a platform of stone or tamped earth. Their heavily tiled roofs were supported by long, stout columns made from single tree-trunks transported from virgin forests in the southwest or northeast. In the larger palace buildings there might be as many as several dozen of these columns.

The tops of the columns were linked by transverse rafters, while elaborate sets of wooden brackets joined the columns to the roof frame (see page 197). The brackets

were constructed of interlocking components that were jointed rather than nailed together. The number and type of brackets would depend on their position in the building, for the roofs were shaped and had upturned overhanging eaves.

The size of a building was measured by the number of spaces (*jian*) between the rafters. Originally, palace buildings were restricted to 9,999 *jian,* because the number 10,000 (*wan*) could only be applied to the emperor, who was sometimes referred to as Lord of Ten Thousand Years (Wan Sui Ye). Apart from this consideration, the number nine was thought to be especially auspicious.

The walls of palace buildings were wattle and daub, and each ceremonial building was painted inside and out. In the case of the Forbidden City and other Ming and Qing palaces, the exterior walls were in red ocher and the beams, rafters, and brackets were painted in elaborate multicolored patterns. The roofs were tiled with golden-yellow flat, glazed tiles, linked together by vertical rows of cylindrical ties. The corners of the roofs were decorated with rows of auspicious pottery beasts (see page 197).

ABOVE
The gilded imperial throne on a raised platform inside the Hall of Supreme Harmony in the Outer Court of the Forbidden City. The Qing broadly left the MIng plan of the palace intact, but renamed a number of the principal buildings. For example, the Hall of Supreme Harmony was originally named the Hall of Imperial Supremacy. Behind the throne is a splendid screen decorated with coiled dragons and on either side of the throne are a crane-shaped candlestick, an elephant-shaped incense burner and a cloisonne-ware column topped with a pagoda.

ABOVE
This bronze tortoise outside the Hall of Supreme Harmony symbolized the wish that the emperor would have a long life and reign.

OPPOSITE, ABOVE
The elaborate internal roof construction of wooden pillars, horizontal rafters, and complex bracketing in the Hall of Supreme Harmony (see page 195).

OPPOSITE, BELOW
A detail of the Forbidden City's typical roofing of golden-yellow tiles, with auspicious beasts on the eaves to deflect evil spirits from the building.

ENTERING THE GREAT WITHIN

The Forbidden City consists of a number of large buildings facing south, in accordance with tradition (south being the chief cardinal point for the Chinese), and arranged on a north–south axis. The main structures are separated by courtyards, on either side of which are auxiliary buildings and smaller buildings such as offices and living quarters. The central axis is flanked by two parallel axes, along which the auxiliary buildings are arranged.

Visitors approaching the Forbidden City from the south first pass through the outer gate, the Tiananmen (Gate of Heavenly Peace). After crossing a courtyard they come to the moat and wall that surrounds the whole palace complex proper, and the main gate, the imposing Wumen (Meridian Gate), originally built in 1420 and later restored. After the Wumen one enters the Outer Palace, crossing the elegantly conduited Golden Water River by one of five marble bridges. To the north is the Outer Court, the largest courtyard in the palace, which contained the offices of the executive arm of government, including the Six Boards (ministries), and all the auxiliary offices of the imperial government. Next, proceeding north, are the Three Ceremonial Halls, one behind the other on the main axis: the Hall of Supreme Harmony, containing the emperor's throne (see page 195), the Hall of Perfect Harmony, and the Hall of the Preservation of Harmony. As their names suggest, the trinity of halls were used exclusively for ceremonial purposes.

North of the halls is the Inner Palace complex. In line with tradition, this is where the Ming and Qing emperors and their families resided, and it also housed the emperor's closest advisors and the imperial guard. Besides his wife, the emperor had a few imperial consorts, usually four in number, as well as many concubines. Because they posed no sexual threat, eunuchs were originally entrusted to attend the female members of the imperial family, but during the Ming and Qing eunuchs acquired many other responsibilities in the imperial household, ranging from handling supplies entering the palace to keeping the imperial seal.

乾隆

THE SETTING SUN

Qianlong and the Later Qing (1735–1912)

OPPOSITE
The Qianlong Emperor in Court Dress, by an anonymous court artist. He wears a robe of the special "bright yellow" (*ming huang*) reserved for imperial garments (see also page 177). Hanging scroll, color on silk, late 18th century.

乾隆

After the death ofYongzheng in 1735, his fourth son, and the favorite grandson of Kangxi, was chosen to succeed. Hongli (1711–1799) took the reign title Qianlong ("Strong and Prosperous"), and reigned for sixty years, abdicating in 1796 only as an act of filial piety—he did not wish to exceed the sixty-one-year reign of his illustrious grandfather. His rule marked the high point of the Qing dynasty's fortunes. During the eighteenth century the Chinese empire covered an area greater than it had ever covered before or since. It included Outer Mongolia and regions of Central Asia and eastern Siberia, which we now think of as parts of the former Soviet Union.

China also increased in wealth and population, thanks largely to a taxation policy that favored small farmers. New crops from the Americas and elsewhere were introduced, such as the groundnut, the sweet potato, and maize, and there was a rapid growth in the production of industrial crops such as tea, cotton, and sugar. Commercial activities flourished and many large and small trade organizations, including guilds, abounded, particularly in the lower Yangzi region. Qianlong made six tours of inspection of the prosperous south, in imitation of Kangxi's own six tours, visiting several southern cities including Suzhou and Hangzhou. Many of these places still have reminders of his visit in the form of commemorative plaques written in the emperor's own hand.

During the second half of the eighteenth century the dynasty's expenditure started to outstrip its income. In spite of this Qianlong was keen to complete ten victorious military campaigns and continued his military operations in northern Turkestan. His inspections of the south also drained much silver from the treasury.

These expenditures, combined with corruption, meant that when Qianlong abdicated he left behind financial problems, which left the dynasty lacking in substantial reserves. In fact, China's zenith under Qianlong was followed by a century of decline. This was to prove disastrous in the nineteenth century when the Qing also had to deal with several large-scale rebellions as well as the increasing incursions of foreign powers.

BELOW
A decorative flattened flask (*bianhu*) from the imperial workshops in Beijing, in the form of an ancient bronze. Copper with *cloisonné* enamel and gilding, Qing dynasty, reign of Qianlong (1735–1796).

ABOVE
Founded in 1884, the Palace of the Heavenly Queen in Yantai, Shandong, is a famous temple dedicated to the popular goddess Mazu, patron of sailors. Yantai was opened to Western nations as a "treaty port" in 1863, and a convention opening additional Chinese ports to foreign trade was signed here in 1876.

OPPOSITE
This carved jade boulder, nearly four feet (114.5 cm) high, depicts the Nine Elders of Huichang, a famous gathering hosted by the Tang poet Bao Juyi for his scholarly friends, who wander through an ideal landscape. A poem by the emperor Qianlong, who owned this piece, extols jade's durability. Green jade (nephrite), dated 1787.

THE RISE OF EUROPEAN INFLUENCE

The key factor in the history of China under the later empire was the increasing presence and influence of other powers. Although the first Christian archbishop of Beijing had died in 1338 when the Mongols ruled China, it was not until after the foundation of the Jesuit order by Ignatius Loyola in 1534 that a new effort was made by the Church to send missionaries to East Asia. After the Portuguese had set up a trading post in Macau it became possible for missions to gain a foothold on the Chinese mainland and the first Jesuit to make his mark was Matteo Ricci, who eventually reached Beijing in 1601.

At first the Christians gained official acceptance by dressing in Buddhist robes, but Ricci soon realized that in order to win over the educated classes he would have to become immersed in Chinese culture. One of his methods was to stress any analogies he could find linking Christianity with Chinese orthodox beliefs, such as using the name of the ancient high god Shangdi (Supreme Lord, see page 21) for the Christian God. The Chinese were also fascinated by Western technical knowledge and mechanical devices, particularly clocks. Eventually Jesuits were employed by the government as astronomers, geographers, and cartographers. Several prominent Chinese scholars were converted and in 1692 Kangxi issued a decree tolerating Christian worship.

會昌九老圖

ABOVE
Kazakhs Presenting Horses to Qianlong as Tribute by Giuseppe Castiglione (1688–1766), known in China as Lang Shining, and anonymous court artists. A Jesuit painter, architect, and missionary, Castiglione arrived in Beijing in 1715 and worked at the imperial court until his death (see page 205). He collaborated with native artists to evolve a distinct combination of Western and Chinese techniques and subjects. Handscroll, ink and color on paper, 1757.

The Jesuits made some headway in China by accepting traditional ancestor rites as a social and not a religious practice, but the Dominicans persuaded the pope to issue a papal bull in 1715 that forbade Chinese Christians to engage in such activities. The Chinese reacted by expelling many missionaries, setting back the cause of conversion.

The Portuguese trading pioneers were followed by the Dutch, who controlled Taiwan for a brief period until expelled by Coxinga in the 1660s (see page 178). The English and French followed later and by the middle of the nineteenth century all the European trading nations as well as Japan and the United States had established a presence in China. The Western powers and Japan sought by every means they could to open up China to free trade, and they did not hesitate to use force when negotiations failed. As a result, in 1842 Hong Kong was ceded to Britain and, later, Taiwan was occupied by Japan. One-sided treaties opened many Chinese ports, such as Shanghai and Tianjin, and granted the Western powers extraterritorial rights, whereby residents of certain areas were subject only to the laws of the occupying power, not the empire.

By then the Qing dynasty was in decline and unable to resist the increasingly acquisitive policies of the foreign powers, or the growing number of rebellions. One of these

was the Taiping Rebellion which began in 1850 and was led at the beginning by a charismatic Christian convert who claimed to be Christ's younger brother. This hugely bloody revolt engulfed much of central and southern China and was only defeated in 1864 by the efforts of Chinese officials loyal to the Manchus leading locally recruited Chinese troops. Thus, as time went on the Manchus relied more and more on Chinese to man and even to command their armies.

THE END OF EMPIRE

Toward the end of the nineteenth century any hopes for political and economic reform were effectively dashed by the ultra-conservative dowager empress Cixi (lived 1835–1908), who effectively governed during the reigns of her son Tongzhi (1862–1875) and nephew Guangxu (1875–1908). Guangxu was sympathetic to the moderate reform movement of 1898 but this ended when Cixi had him placed under house arrest. The dowager empress wasted precious funds to finance her supreme folly, a new Summer Palace near Beijing. Disastrously, she also supported the Boxer Rising of 1899–1901, which saw attacks on the foreign legations. With modernization of the military one area

ABOVE
Putuo Zongcheng, the "Little Potala," a Buddhist temple and palace erected 1767–1771 by the emperor Qianlong at Chengde, the imperial summer retreat in the hills 100 miles (160 km) northeast of Beijing. Built between 1703 and 1789, the vast retreat incorporates a number of structures in the style of the monumental buildings of Lhasa, the capital of Tibet and seat of the Dalai Lamas, of whom the Qing emperors were patrons.

of reform persistently blocked by Cixi's profligacy, the Qing armies proved no match when troops of seven Western powers (the United States, Britain, Russia, Germany, Austria, France, Italy) and Japan invaded China and occupied Tianjin and Beijing.

These allies imposed financial indemnities that hastened the demise of the dynasty. The end came swiftly following the death of both Cixi and Guangxu in 1908, leaving a boy, Xuantong (Puyi), on the throne. With revolts widespread, in 1911 reformers took over the government and declared a republic. In 1912 Puyi abdicated, but he was allowed to remain in the imperial palace until 1924 (he ended his days as a humble gardener in Beijing, where he died in 1967). Thus the Manchu dynasty, and with it more than two thousand years of imperial rule, came to an end with barely a whimper.

ART AND LITERATURE OF THE LATER QING

Qianlong was a notable patron of the arts, and he supported a number of court painters. He admired the European style of the Italian Jesuit painter Giuseppe Castiglione (1688–1766) and commissioned paintings from him of landscapes, court and military ceremonies, figures on horseback, and other subjects (see illustration, pages 202–203).

Qianlong also employed several Jesuit missionaries in the construction of the old Summer Palace—known originally as the Qingyi Yuan (Garden of Clear Ripples)—on the outskirts of Beijing, from 1750 to 1765. The palace was later pillaged and burnt by Anglo-French armies in 1860 to persuade the Chinese government to grant full diplomatic relations and more facilities for international trade; however, its "Sino-Baroque" style is still evident from the surviving ruins.

Castiglione's collaboration with court artists on a number of works introduced strong European elements to Chinese painting, particularly with regard to shading and perspective. Outside the court, traditional painting continued to develop and during the Qianlong period the individualist trend of the early Qing was maintained by a group known as the "Eight Eccentrics of Yangzhou," a prospering city in Jiangsu, eastern China, whose salt merchants and others presented artists with a middle-class market and where the early Qing artist Shi Tao (see pages 184–186) had spent his final years. The Eccentrics—Wang Shishen (1686–1759), Huang Shen (1687–1768), Li Shan (ca. 1686–1756), Jin Nong (1687–1764), Gao Xiang (1688–1753), Zheng Xie (1693–1765), Li Fangying (1696–1755), and Luo Pin (1733–1799)—were aesthetes, often from backgrounds of poverty, who abandoned the struggle for wealth and rank in order to be free to express their true feelings in their paintings. The Eccentrics' typical paintings were of plum blossoms (Wang Shishen was especially noted for these), lilies, bamboos, pines, and rocks, though Huang Shen (1687–1772), who came originally from Fujian, specialized in human figures such as fisherfolk, silk weavers, and beggars.

It was also an era of great literature and two novels were written that are acknowledged to be masterpieces of their respective genres. The first, translated into English as *A Dream of Red Mansions* or *The Story of The Stone*, was by Cao Xueqin, the descendant of one of the richest families in China, who owned the silk factories that produced garments for the imperial court. The novel is a detailed account of daily life in a house of many courtyards and gardens inhabited by a large extended family of many dozens of members with countless servants. Of the hundreds of characters, several dozen stand out as unforgettable people, each with his or her individuality,

BELOW
An intricate octagonal (eight is an auspicious number in Chinese culture) filigree box decorated with dragon motifs demonstrates the skill of Chinese metal craftsmen in the Qing dynasty. Silver and gold, 18th or 19th century.

ABOVE
Elaborate earrings such as these were worn by wealthy Chinese women as a sign of status. Silver with blue enamel, Qing dynasty, late 18th-early 19th century.

OPPOSITE
Women became a popular subject for artists during the Qing era. *Lu Zhu Composing a Poem* is a painting from *Ten Famous Women*, an album by Sun Huang (flourished mid-18th century). Ink and color on silk, dated 1757.

FOLLOWING PAGES
A table top depicting a scholar and attendants in a pavilion by a river. Scholars in rustic settings were a favorite subject down the ages. Carved red lacquer, Qing dynasty, ca. 18th century.

whether they be family or servants. The second novel, by Wu Jingzi, translates as *The Scholars* and it is China's outstanding satirical novel. Wu Jingzi was extremely critical of the state examination system, which by that time concentrated on the candidates' ability to write essays to a set pattern based on the ideology of the Neoconfucians of the Song dynasty. Some of the products of this system remained basically ignorant and unfit to serve as officials. Wu Jingzi was merciless towards them, but usually his satire was quite subtle and based on a sharp and critical intellect.

During the last two decades of the Qing Dynasty many more satirical novels were published, often serially in magazines printed by the new machine presses, which by now were also producing the first popular newspapers. Times were changing rapidly.

TOWARD A NEW CALLIGRAPHY

An important cultural activity under the Qing was "research based on evidence" (*kaozheng xue*), whereby scholars sought to authenticate ancient writings by making detailed comparisons with inscriptions on stone stelae and bronze ritual vessels. This rigorous study was partly a response to a discouraging attitude toward independent

thinking under the early Qing rulers, but one effect it had was to stimulate experimentation with calligraphy. Part of this revival took the form of a conscious criticism of post-Han masters whose style had been so revered as to have stifled innovation. A particular target was the great Wang Xizhi, whose influence first came under criticism from Jin Nong, one of the Eight Eccentrics of Yangzhou, who evolved a "heretical" calligraphic style with block-like characters drawn in thick ink with a clipped brush, as opposed to the elegantly tapered style of Wang Xizhi and others.

OPPOSITE
The Jade Belt Bridge, built out of marble and white stone (1751–1764) on Lake Kunming within the grounds of the imperial Summer Palace in Beijing. The railings are adorned with cranes and the high, single arch was designed to accommodate the dragon boat of the emperor Qianlong.

TRADITION AND EXPERIMENT IN THE LATE EMPIRE

From the reign of Qianlong to the end of the empire, innovation took place in the world of art alongside the continued production of quality works in traditional styles, genres, and subjects. Noted artists included Fei Danxu (or Zitiao, 1802–1850), who worked mainly in Jiangsu and Zhejiang provinces and was renowned for his human figures. The foreign market played a role in stimulating activity in the southern port of Guangzhou (Canton), home of Lam Qua (Guan Qiaochang/Kwan Kiu Cheong in Cantonese; 1801–1860), who became famous for his Western-style oil portraits. In the 1820s Lam Qua had studied in Macau under Englishman George Chinnery (1774–1852), probably the only European professional artist working in China in the first half of the nineteenth century.

From the mid-nineteenth century, the dominant city of the lower Yangzi was Shanghai, newly opened to Western trade under the Treaty of Nanjing, which ended the First Opium War of 1839–1842. Ren Xiong (1820–1857) and Ren Yi (or Ren Bonian, 1840–1896) were prominent among the period's flourishing "Shanghai School" of artists. They and others of the school often had traditional *literati* backgrounds and generally respected the techniques and styles of the old masters. But under the influence of Western ideas their works often break with *literati* tradition in introducing new subjects and themes, a new boldness in the use of color, and an element of social critique. Shanghai artists produced fewer landscapes, and more portraits, than their predecessors. Working at a time of profound change, of transition, and within an atmosphere of contrasts, the professional artists of Shanghai anticipated the radical modernizing movements China was to embrace in the twentieth century.

BELOW
This barrel-shaped *famille verte cloisonné* porcelain object is a garden stool of a type that became popular in the later empire. Qing dynasty.

GLOSSARY

accouterment Equipment or clothing, part of an outfit.
anachronistic Out of place chronologically.
basin A depression in the land surface.
calligraphy The art of producing elegant, ornamental writing.
dialect A regional variety of language, distinguished by grammar, vocabulary, and pronunciation.
earthenware Dishes made from clay and fired at low heat.
mausoleum A large above-ground tomb.
missionary A person undertaking a religious mission.
monopoly Exclusive ownership or control of a particular market.
motif A dominant theme.
nomad One who has no fixed residence, but travels from place to place, usually following a food supply.
smelting To melt or fuse minerals to separate the metal.
terracotta Fired clay used for building statues or architectural ornamentation.

FOR MORE INFORMATION

British Museum
Great Russell Street
London, UK WC1B 3DG
+44 (0)20 7323 8299
Web site: http://www.britishmuseum.org
A museum with a large array of art and artifacts from throughout human history.

Chinese American Museum
125 Paseo de la Plaza, Suite 300
Los Angeles, CA 90012
Web site: http://www.camla.org
Museum dedicated to fostering a deeper understanding and appreciation of America's diverse heritage by researching, preserving, and sharing the history, rich cultural legacy, and continuing contributions of Chinese Americans.

Chinese Historical Society of America Museum
965 Clay Street
San Francisco, CA 94108
Web site: http://www.chsa.org
CHSA is the oldest and largest organization in the country dedicated to the documentation, study, and presentation of Chinese American history.

Metropolitan Museum of Art
1000 Fifth Avenue
New York, New York 10028-0198
(212) 535-7710
Web site: http://www.metmuseum.org
One of the world's largest and finest art museums with collections that include more than two million works of art spanning five thousand years of world culture, from prehistory to the present and from every part of the globe.

University of California, San Diego
Chinese Studies Program
9500 Gilman Drive, MC 0104
Humanities & Social Sciences Building, Rm. 3084
La Jolla, CA 92093-0104
Web site: http://chinesestudies.ucsd.edu

An interdisciplinary program that allows students interested in China to utilize the university's offerings in various departments to build an interdisciplinary major leading to a B.A. degree.

University of Washington
China Studies Program
East Asia Studies
Box 353650
Seattle, WA 98195
Web site: http://jsis.washington.edu/china/
The China Studies Program in the Henry M. Jackson School of International Studies is an interdisciplinary designed to give students a broad knowledge of the history, sociology, politics, and language of China.

Web Sites

Due to the changing nature of Internet links, Rosen Publishing has developed an online list of Web sites related to the subject of this book. This site is updated regularly. Please use this link to access the list:

http://www.rosenlinks.com/ANWR/China

FOR FURTHER READING

Anderson, Dale. *Ancient China.* Mankato, MN: Heinemann-Raintree, 2005.

Anderson, Jameson. *The History and Activities of Ancient China.* Mankato, MN: Heinemann-Raintree, 2006.

Ball, Jacqueline. *National Geographic Investigates: Ancient China.* Des Moines, IA: National Geographic Children's Books. 2006.

Collins, Terry. *Ancient China: An Interactive History Adventure.* North Mankato, MN: Capstone, 2012.

Cotterell, Arthur. *Ancient China.* New York, NY: DK, 2005.

Dubois, Muriel L. *Ancient China: Beyond the Great Wall.* North Mankato, MN: Capstone, 2011.

Friedman, Mel. *Ancient China.* Danbury, CT: Children's Press, 2010.

If I Were a Kid in Ancient China: Children of the Ancient World. Peterborough, NH: Cobblestone, 2007.

Kramer, Lance. *Great Ancient China Projects You Can Build Yourself.* White River Junction, VT: Nomad Press, 2008.

Lewis, Mark Edward. *The Early Chinese Empires: Qin and Han.* Cambridge, MA: Belknap Press, 2010.

Schomp, Virginia. *The Ancient Chinese.* Danbury, CT: Children's Press, 2005.

Sebaq-Montefiore, Hugh. *China.* New York, NY: DK, 2007.

Shuter, Jane. *Ancient China.* Mankato, MN: Heinemann-Raintree, 2007.

BIBLIOGRAPHY

GENERAL HISTORIES AND REFERENCE

Birrell, A. *Chinese Mythology: An Introduction.* Johns Hopkins University Press: Baltimore and London, 1993.

Blunden, C., and M. Elvin. *A Cultural Atlas of China.* Facts on File: New York, 1998.

Boyd, A. *Chinese Architecture and Town Planning 1500BC–AD1911.* Alec Tiranti: London, 1962.

Cahill, J. *Chinese Painting.* (Treasures of Asia Series) Macmillan: London, 1977.

de Crespigny, R.C. *China: The Land and its People.* Thomas Nelson: Melbourne, 1971.

Fairbank, J.K., and M. Goldman. *China: A New History*, 2nd enlarged edition. Harvard University Press (HUP): Cambridge, Mass., 2005.

Fairbank, J.K., and D.C. Twitchett, gen. eds. *The Cambridge History of China.* 15 vols. covering 221 BCE–the present. Cambridge University Press (CUP): Cambridge, England, and New York, USA, 1979–. The most complete history of China in English.

Fung Yu-lan (Feng Youlan). *A History of Chinese Philosophy*, trans. D. Bodde, 2 vols. Princeton University Press: Princeton, New Jersey, and Allen and Unwin: London, 1952 (in paperback, 1983).

Gernet, J. *A History of Chinese Civilization.* CUP: New York, 1996.

Hook, B., and D.C. Twitchett, eds. *The Cambridge Encyclopaedia of China.* CUP: Cambridge, England, 1982.

Lee, S.E., and H. Rogers, eds. *China: 5,000 Years – Innovation and Transformation in the Arts.* Guggenheim Museum: New York, 1998.

Loewe, M. *The Pride That Was China.* Sidgwick and Jackson: London, 1990.

Medley, M. *Handbook of Chinese Art.* Bell and Sons: London, 1977.

Nagel's Encyclopaedia-Guide China. Nagel Publishers: Geneva, 1984. Section *"Peking"*(pp.400–649) includes notes on the history and function of the Imperial Palace and the Temple of Heaven.

Needham, J., gen ed. *Science and Civilisation in China.* 7 vols. CUP: Cambridge, England, and New York, USA, 1956–. Monumental study of Chinese science, technology, and society.

Shaughnessy, E.L. (gen. ed.) *China: Land of the Heavenly Dragon.* Published in the US as *China: Empire and Civilization.* Duncan Baird Publishers: London, and Oxford University Press (OUP): New York, 2000.

Temple, R. *The Genius of China: 3,000 Years of Science, Discovery and Invention.* Simon and Schuster: New York, 1986, and Prion Books: London, 1998.

Tregear, T.R. *A Geography of China.* University of London Press: London, 1965.

Watson, W. *The Arts of China.* 3 vols. (vol. 3 written with Chumei Ho). Yale University Press (YUP): New Haven, 2000–2007.

CHAPTER ONE

Chang Kwang-chih. *Shang Civilization.* (4th ed.) YUP: New Haven and London, 1987.

Chuang-tzu (Zhuangzi), trans. A.C.. Graham. *The Chuang-tzu.* Unwin Paperbacks: London, 1986

Confucius, trans. D.C. Lau. *The Analects.* Penguin Books: Harmondsworth, England, and New York, USA, 1979.

Hawkes, D., trans. *The Songs of the South*. Penguin Books: Harmondsworth, England, 1985.
Hsu Cho-yun. *Ancient China in Transition*. Stanford University Press: Stanford, 1965.
Keightley, D.N. *Sources of Shang History: The Oracle-bone Inscriptions of Bronze Age China*. University of California Press: Berkeley and London, 1978
Lau, D.C., trans. *The Tao Te Ching*. Penguin Books: Harmondsworth, England, 1963.
Li Xueqin, trans. K.C. Chang. *Eastern Zhou and Qin Civilizations*. YUP: New Haven and London, 1985.
Li Xueqin. *The Wonder of Chinese Bronzes*. Foreign Languages Press: Beijing, 1980.
Loewe, M., and E.L. Shaughnessy. *The Cambridge History of Ancient China*. CUP: Cambridge, England, and New York, 1999.
Companion to the *Cambridge History of China*, covering the period to 221 BCE.
Mencius (Mengzi), trans. D.C. Lau. *The Mencius*. Penguin Books: Harmondsworth, England, and New York, 1970.
Rawson, Jessica. *Ancient China: Art and Archaeology*. British Museum Press: London, 1980.
Rawson, J. *Chinese Jade from the Neolithic to the Qing*. British Museum Press: London, 1995.
Rawson, J., ed. *Mysteries of Ancient China: New Discoveries from the Ancient Dynasties*. British Museum Press: London, 1996.
Waley, A., trans. *The Book of Songs*. Allen and Unwin: London, 1937.
Waley, A. *Three Ways of Thought in Ancient China*. Allen and Unwin: London, 1939.
Watson, W. *China*. (Ancient People and Places series.) Thames and Hudson: London, 1966.
Wen Fong, ed. *The Great Bronze Age of China*. Metropolitan Museum of Art/Knopf: New York, 1980.

CHAPTER TWO

Birrel, A., trans. *New Songs from a Jade Terrace, An Anthology of Early Chinese Love Poetry*. Penguin Books: Harmondsworth, England, 1986.
Bodde, D. *China's First Unifier: A Study of the Ch'in Dynasty as Seen in the Life of Li Ssu, 280–208BC*. E.J. Brill: Leiden, Netherlands, 1938 (reprinted Hong Kong University Press: Hong Kong, 1967).
de Crespigny, R.C. *The Last of the Han*. Australian National University Press: Canberra, 1969.
Forke, A., trans. *Lun Heng: Wang Ch'ung's Essays*. 2 vols. Paragon Book Gallery: New York, 1962.
Gale, E. *Discourses on Salt and Iron*. E.J. Brill: Leiden, Netherlands, 1934. (Continued in journal of the North China Branch of the Royal Asiatic Society, LXV pp.73–110.)
Ledderose, L. "A Magic Army for the Emperor" in Ledderose, L., ed. *Ten Thousand Things: Module Mass Production in Chinese Art*. Princeton University Press: Princeton, New Jersey, 2000.
Loewe, M. *Records of Han Administration*. 2 vols. CUP: Cambridge, England, 1967.
Loewe, M. *Everyday Life in Early Imperial China*. Batsford: London, 1968.
Loewe, M. *Crisis and Conflict in Han China, 104BC to 9AD*. Allen and Unwin: London, 1974.
Sima Qian, trans. R. Dawson. *Historical Records*. Oxford and New York, Oxford University Press, 1994. Early Chinese account of the First Emperor.
Twitchett, D.C., and M. Loewe, eds. *The Cambridge History of China, vol. 1: The Ch'in and Han Empires, 221BC to AD220*. CUP: Cambridge, England, 1994.
Watson, B. *Records of the Grand Historian of China*. 2 vols. Columbia University Press: New York and London, 1961.

CHAPTER THREE

Bai Ziran, ed. *Dazu Grottoes*. Foreign Language Press: Beijing, 1984.
Casewell, J.O. *A New History of the Buddhist Caves of Yungang*. University of British Columbia Press: Vancouver, 1988.
Eberhard, W. *Conquerors and Rulers, Social Forces in Medieval China*. E.J. Brill: Leiden, Netherlands, 1965.
Fairbank, J.K., ed. *The Chinese World Order: Traditional China's Foreign Relations*. HUP: Cambridge, Mass., 1968.
Fang, A. *The Chronicle of the Three Kingdoms* (AD 220–265). 2 vols. HUP: Cambridge, Mass., 1962 and 1965.
Fujieda, A. "The Tun-Huan Manuscripts," in Leslie, D., C. Mackerras and Wang Gungwu, eds. *Essays on the Sources for Chinese History*. Australian National University Press: Canberra, 1973.
Gray, B. *Buddhist Cave Paintings at Tunhuang*. University of Chicago Press: Chicago, 1959.
Hopkirk, P. *Foreign Devils on the Silk Road: The Search for the Lost Cities and Treasures of Chinese Central Asia*. University of Massachusetts Press: Amhurst, Mass., 1990.
Kieschnick, J. *The Impact of Buddhism on Chinese National Culture*. Princeton University Press: Princeton, New Jersey, 2003.
Lattimore, O. *Inner Asian Frontiers of China*. Beacon Press: Boston, Mass., 1962.
McCausland, S. *First Masterpiece of Chinese Painting: The Admonitions Scroll*. British Museum Press: London, 2003.
Ning Qiang. *Art, Religion and Politics in Medieval China: The Dunhuang Cave of the Zhai Family*. University of Hawai'i Press: Honolulu, 2004.
Paludan, A. *Chinese Tomb Figurines*. OUP: New York, 1994.
Wright, A. *Buddhism in Chinese History*. Stanford University Press: Stanford, 1959.
Zürcher, E. *The Buddhist Conquest of China: The Spread and Adaptation of Buddhism in Medieval China*. 2 vols. E.J. Brill: Leiden, Netherlands, 1959.

CHAPTER FOUR

Benn, C. *Everyday Life in the Tang Dynasty*. OUP: Oxford, 2002.
Bernstein, R. *Ultimate Journey: Retracing the Path of an Ancient Buddhist Monk who Crossed Asia in Search of Enlightenment*. Knopf: New York, 2001.
Bielenstein, H. *Diplomacy and Trade in the Chinese World, 589–1276*. E.J. Brill: Leiden, Netherlands, and Boston, Mass., 2005.
Bingham, W. *The Founding of the T'ang*. Waverly Press: Baltimore, 1941.
Carter, T.F. *The Invention of Printing in China and its Spread Westward*. Ronald Press: New York, 1955.
Fitzgerald, C.P. *The Empress Wu*. University of British Columbia Press: Vancouver, 1968.
Fitzgerald, C.P. *Son of Heaven: A Biography of Li Shih- min*. CUP: Cambridge, England, 1933.
Keim, J.A. *Chinese Art: From the Beginning to the T'ang Dynasty*. Methuen: London, 1961.
Li Po and Tu Fu, trans. Arthur Cooper. *Poems*. Penguin Books: Harmondsworth, England, 1973
McMullen, D. *State and Scholars in Tang China*. CUP: Cambridge, England, 1988.

Pulleyblank, E.G. *The Background of the Rebellion of An Lu-shan*. OUP: Oxford, 1955, and Greenwood Press: Westport, Conn., 1982.
Twitchett, D.C. *Financial Administration under the T'ang Dynasty*. CUP: Cambridge, England, 1963.
Twitchett, D.C., ed. *The Cambridge History of China, vol.3: Sui and T'ang, 589–906AD*. CUP: Cambridge, England, and New York, USA, 1979.
Waley, A. *The Life and Times of Po Chü-yi*. Allen and Unwin: London, 1949.
Watson, W. *The Arts of China to AD900*. YUP: New Haven, 2000.
Wright, A.F. *The Sui Dynasty*. Knopf: New York, 1978.

CHAPTER FIVE

Chang, C. *The Development of Neo-Confucian Thought*. Vision Press: London, 1958.
Chiang Yee. *Chinese Calligraphy*. Methuen: London, 1961.
Ecke, Tseng Yu-ho. *Chinese Calligraphy.* Philadelphia Museum of Art: Philadelphia, 1971.
Gernet, J. *Daily Life in China on the Eve of the Mongol Invasion*. Macmillan: New York, 1967.
Keim, J.A. *Chinese Art II: The Five Dynasties and Northern Sung*. Methuen: London, 1961.
Kracke, E.A., Jr. *The Civil Service in Early Sung China*. HUP: Cambridge, Mass., 1953.
Lin Yutang. *The Gay Genius: The Life and Times of Su Tung-po*. J. Day: New York, 1947.
Liu, J.T.C. *Reform in Sung China, Wang An-shih and his New Policies*. HUP: Cambridge, Mass., 1959.
Liu, J.T.C. *Ou-yang Hsiu: An Eleventh century Neo-Confucianist*. Stanford University Press: Stanford, 1967.
Twitchett, D.C., and H. Franke, eds. *The Cambridge History of China, vol.6: The Alien Regimes and Border States, 710–1368*. CUP: Cambridge, England, and New York, 1994.
Wang Gung-wu. *The Structure of Power in North China During the Five Dynasties*. University of Malaya Press: Kuala Lumpur, 1963, and Stanford University Press: Stanford, 1967.

CHAPTER SIX

Dreyer, E.L. *Early Ming China: A Political History, 1355–1435*. Stanford University Press: Stanford, 1982.
Ho Ping-ti. *The Ladder of Success in Imperial China: Aspects of Social Mobility, 1368–1911*. Columbia University Press: New York and London, 1962.
Hobson, R.L. *The Wares of the Ming Dynasty*. Dover Publications: New York, 1978.
Hucker, C.O. *The Censorial System of Ming China*, Stanford University Press: Stanford, 1966.
Hucker, C.O. *The Traditional Chinese State in Ming Times (1368–1644)*. University of Arizona Press: Tucson, 1961
Langlois, J.D., ed. *China Under Mongol Rule*. Princeton University Press: Princeton, New Jersey, 1981.
Levathes, L. *When China Ruled the Seas*. Simon and Schuster: New York, 1994.

Luo Guanzhong, trans. Moss Roberts. *Three Kingdoms*. University of California Press: Berkeley and Los Angeles, 1999,
Medley, M. *The Chinese Potter: A Practical History of Chinese Ceramics*. Phaidon: Oxford, 1976.
Mote, S.W., and D.C. Twitchett, eds. *The Cambridge History of China, vol.7: The Ming Dynasty*. CUP: Cambridge, 1988.
Neave-Hill, W.B.R. *Chinese Ceramics*. John Bartholomew: Edinburgh and London, 1975.
Paladan, A. *The Ming Tombs*. OUP: Oxford, 1991.
Rossabi, M. *Khubilai Khan: His Life and Times*. University of California Press: Berkeley, Los Angeles, and London, 1988.
Shi Nai'an, trans. Sidney Shapiro. *Outlaws of the Marsh*, 4 vols. Foreign Languages Press: Beijing, 1980 (paperback edition 2005).
Wu Chengen, trans. W.J.F. Jenner. *The Journey to the West*. 4 vols. Foreign Languages Press: Beijing and University of Chicago Press: Chicago and London, 1977–1986.

CHAPTER SEVEN

Ch'ü T'ung-tsu. *Local Government in China under the Ch'ing*. HUP: Cambridge, Mass., 1968.
Fairbank, J.K., ed. *The Cambridge History of China vol.10: The Late Ch'ing, 1800–1911, Part 1*. CUP: Cambridge, England, and New York, 1978.
Fairbank, J.K., and Kwang-Ching Liu, eds. *The Cambridge History of China vol.11: The Late Ch'ing, 1800–1911, Part 2*. CUP: Cambridge and New York, 1980.
Heath, I., and M. Perry. *The Taiping Rebellions 1851–1866*. Reed International Books Ltd.: London, 1994.
Johnson, R.F. *Twilight in the Forbidden City*. OUP: New York, 1985.
Kerr, R. *Chinese Ceramics: Porcelain of the Qing Dynasty 1644–1911*. Victoria and Albert Museum: London, 1998.
Levenson, J.R. *Confucian China and its Modern Fate: The Problem of Intellectual Continuity*. Routledge and Kegan Paul: London, 1958.
Peterson, W.J., ed. *The Cambridge History of China vol.9: The Ch'ing Dynasty to 1800, Part 1*. CUP: Cambridge and New York, 2002.
Perdue, P. *China Marches West. The Qing Conquest of Central Eurasia*. HUP: Cambridge, Mass., 2006.
Preston, Diane. *The Boxer Rebellion*. Berkeley Publishing Group: California, 1988.
Spence, J., and J. Wills Jr, eds. *From Ming to Qing: Conquest, Region and Continuity in 17th century China*. YUP: New Haven, 1979.
Wakeman, F. *Strangers at the Gate: Social Disorder in South China 1839-1861*. University of California Press: Berkeley, 1997.
Waley, A. *The Opium War through Chinese Eyes*. Allen and Unwin: London, 1958.
Wright, M.C. *The Last Stand of Chinese Conservatism: The T'ung-chih Restoration, 1862–74*. Atheneum: New York, 1966.

INDEX

References in *italics* are to picture captions.

ACKNOWLEDGMENTS AND PICTURE CREDITS

ACKNOWLEDGMENTS
To my wife Ying for her support.

PICTURE CREDITS
The publisher would like to thank the following people, museums, and photographic libraries for permission to reproduce their material. Every care has been taken to trace copyright holders. However, if we have omitted anyone we apologize and will, if informed, make corrections to any future edition.

AA = Art Archive, London
AKG = AKG-images, London
BAL = Bridgeman Art Library, London
BM = © Trustees of the British Museum, London. All rights reserved
CRP = Cultural Relics Publishing House, Beijing
HIP = Heritage Image Partnership, London
HKCTP = Hong Kong China Tourism Press, Quarry Bay, Hong Kong
MEAA = Museum of East Asian Art, Bath
MG = Musée Guimet, Paris
NPM = National Palace Museum, Taipei
PM = © The Palace Museum, Beijing
RMN = Réunion des Musées Nationaux, Paris
ROM = Royal Ontario Museum, Toronto
WFA = Werner Forman Archive, London
(l= left), (r = right), (t = top), (b = bottom)

Page 1 MG/Photo RMN - ©Jean-Gilles Berizzi; **2** HKCTP; **3** Scala, Florence/HIP/MEAA; **4 & 6** BM; **7** Corbis/Tiziana and Gianni Baldizzone; **8** BM; **10** MG/Photo RMN – ©Droits réservés; **11** BM; **12–13** MG/Photo RMN – ©Thierry Ollivier; **14** CRP/Historical Museum, Beijing; **15** CRP/Institute of Archaeology, Qinghai; **16** Corbis/Asian Art & Archaeology, Inc/Institute of Archaeology, Beijing; **17** CRP/Institute of Archaeology, Beijing; **18** BM; **19** Corbis/Asian Art & Archaeology, Inc; **20** Mainstream images/Institute of Archaeology, Beijing; **21** BM; **22** Mainstream images/BM; **23** BM; **24** MG/Photo RMN – ©Richard Lambert; **25** Christie's Images, London; **26** MG/Photo RMN – ©Ravaux; **26** Corbis/ROM; **27** Christie's Images, London; **28** Corbis/Francis G. Mayer; **30–31** Getty images/Image Bank/DreamPictures; **32** Panos/Georg Gerster; **33** Corbis/ROM; **34** BM; **35** Corbis/Asian Art & Archaeology, Inc; **36** AKG/Laurent Lecat; 37 Corbis/Keren Su; **38**, **39** l & r & **40** Araldo de Luca, Rome; **41** Index sas, Florence; **42–43** CRP/Hebei Provincial Museum, Wuhan; **43** CRP/National Museum of Chinese History, Beijing; **44** MG/Photo RMN – ©Thierry Ollivier; **45** CRP/Hunan Provincial Museum, Changsha; **46** Corbis/Asian Art & Archaeology, Inc; **47** CRP/Museum of Jiangchuan County, Yunnan; **48** AKG/ Erich Lessing; **49** CRP/Sichuan Provincial Museum, Chengdu; **50** Mainstream images/Henan Provincial Museum, Zhengzhou; **51** Mainstream images/Cultural Relics Bureau, Xindu county, Sichuan; **52** CRP/Sichuan Provincial Museum, Chengdu; **53** WFA/PM; **54–55** WFA; **56–57** CRP/National Museum of Chinese History, Beijing; **57** CRP/Institute of Archaeology, Anhui; **58** CRP/Administrative Office for Cultural Relics of Anxiang county, Hunan; **59** CRP/Museum of Xinjiang Uyguyr Autonomous Region; **60** Christie's Images, London; **61** CRP/ Museum of Xinjiang Uyguyr Autonomous Region; **62** CRP/Datong Municipal Museum, Shanxi; **63 & 64** MG/ Photo RMN – ©Daniel Arnaudet; **65** Christie's Images, London; **66 & 67** WFA; **68** MG/Photo RMN - ©Richard Lambert; **69** Qingzhou Municipal Museum, Shangdong Province. Photo: The State Administration of Cultural Heritage, People's Republic of China; **70** l Corbis/Tibor Bognar; **70** r WFA; **71** Corbis/Pierre Colombel; **72** Alamy/George Brice; **74 & 75** HKCTP; **76** Alamy/Fenix Rising; **77** Alamy/Dennis Cox; **78–79** AA/MG/Dagli Orti; **80** BM; **81** AA/Bibliothèque Nationale, Paris; **82** Corbis/Pierre Colombel; **84** WFA/Michael B. Weisbrod Inc, New York; **85** WFA/NPM; **86** AA/Genius of China Exhibition; **87** Corbis/ROM; **88** BAL/Museum of Fine Arts, Boston, Massachusetts, Denman Waldo Ross Collection; **89** MG/Photo RMN – ©Robert Asselberghs; **90** l David Lyons; **90** r Corbis/Lowell Georgia; **91** WFA; **92** Corbis/Lowell Georgia; **93** CRP; **94 & 95** MG/Photo RMN – ©Thierry Ollivier; **96** WFA/Eskenazi Ltd, London; **97** WFA/Idemitsu Museum of Arts, Tokyo; **98–99** WFA/NPM; 100 WFA; **101** BM; **102** Corbis/Asian Art & Archaeology, Inc; **103** MG/Photo RMN – ©Richard Lambert; **104–105** BAL/Museum of Fine Arts, Boston, Massachusetts, Maria Antoinette Evans Fund; **106** WFA; **107** AA/MG/Dagli Orti; **108** CRP/Institute of Archaeology, Inner Mongolia Autonomous Region; **109** MG/ Photo RMN – ©Jean-Yves et Nicolas Dubois; **110–111** t BM; **111** b MG/Photo RMN – ©Thierry Ollivier; **112–113** t PM; **113** b Percival David Foundation of Chinese Art, London; **114** MG/Photo RMN – ©Daniel Arnaudet; **115** MG/Photo RMN – ©Jean-Yves et Nicolas Dubois; **116** MG/Photo RMN – ©Droits réservés; **117** l MG/ Photo RMN – ©Richard Lambert; **118–119 & 119 r** Photolibrary.com; **120** CRP/Yunnan Provincial Museum; **121** BAL/Private Collection/Paul Freeman; **122, 123, 124–125** NPM; **126** BAL/Private Collection; **127** Daitoku-ji, Kyoto; **128–129** MG/Photo RMN – ©Thierry Ollivier; **130–131** NPM; **132** t AKG/NPM; **133** BAL/Brooklyn Museum of Art, New York, William E. Hutchins Collection; **134–135** BM; **136** MG/Photo RMN - ©Richard Lambert; **137** MG/Photo RMN – ©Thierry Ollivier; **138** WFA/Christian Deydier, London; **139** MG/Photo RMN – ©Richard Lambert; **140** t & b Percival David Foundation of Chinese Art, London; **141** WFA/courtesy Spink, London; **142 & 143** MG/Photo RMN – ©Thierry Ollivier; **144** BAL/NPM; **145** BM; **146** WFA/Private Collection; **147** MG/Photo RMN – ©Thierry Ollivier; **148–149** Victoria & Albert Museum, London/V&A images; **150** Corbis/Asian Art & Archaeology, Inc; **151** AKG/Private Collection/François Guénet; **152** AKG/ Bruce Connolly; **153** BM; **154** WFA/Private Collection; **155** AKG/Private Collection/François Guénet; **156** Scala, Florence/HIP/MEAA; **157** Christie's Images, London; **158** Alamy/David Ball; **159** Corbis/Dean Conger; **160** l SuperStock/AGE fotostock; **160** r Alamy/Dennis Cox; **161** Corbis/Liu Liqun; **162 & 163** Christie's Images, London; **164** Scala, Florence/HIP/MEAA; **165** BAL/Private Collection/Paul Freeman; **166** Alamy/SAS; **167** MG/Photo RMN – ©Ghislain Vanneste; **168 & 169** Corbis/ROM; **170–171** Alamy/Stuart Aspey; **172** l Alamy/

Hemis; **172** r Corbis/Eye Ubiquitous/James Davis; **173** Alamy/Jon Bower; **174–175** Getty images/Image Bank/ Yann Layma; **176, 177, 178 & 179** PM; **180–181** BAL/British Library, London; **182–183** PM; **184–185** MG/ Photo RMN – ©Ghislain Vanneste; **186** BAL/Private Collection; **187** MG/Photo RMN – ©Jean-Gilles Berizzi; **189** BM; **190** b Alamy/Panorama Media (Beijing) Ltd; **191** PM; **192–193** HKCTP; **194** WFA; **195** Corbis/ Alfred Ko; **196** Photolibrary.com/Jtb Photo Communications Inc; **197** t Alamy/Felix Stensson; **197** b Alamy/ John Henshall; **198 & 199** PM; **200** t David Lyons; **201** PM; **202–203** MG/Photo RMN – ©Droits réservés; **204** Alamy/AM Corporation; **205** Scala, Florence/HIP/MEAA; **206** WFA/Private Collection; **207** MG/Photo RMN – ©Ghislain Vanneste; **208–209** Christie's Images, London; **210** HKCTP; **211** BAL/Private Collection/Paul Freeman

Chapter opener captions

12–13 An engraved bronze *hu* (detail), Eastern Zhou.

30–31 The Great Wall of China.

54–55 Giant stone-carved Buddha at Yungang.

78–79 Tang-dynasty era painted silk of a *boddhisatva*, from Mogao caves, Dunhuang (detail).

104–105 *Five-colored Parakeet on a Blossoming Apricot Tree* by Emperor Huizong. Northern Song, ca. 1110.

128–129 Ming-dynasty embroidered fragment.

174–175 Imperial lion in the Forbidden City.

ABOUT THE AUTHOR

John Chinnery is a former Head of the Department of East Asian Studies at Edinburgh University, Scotland, where he lectured on the History of Chinese Civilization. He was a founding member, and is now Honorary President, of the Scotland China Association. His first visit to China was in 1954, as part of a cultural delegation to the newly founded People's Republic of China, which was cordially received by the Chinese Premier Zhou Enlai. He witnessed the Great Leap Forward firsthand, but was unable to visit China again until after the Cultural Revolution. Since then, he has been an annual visitor. He has written many articles about China for academic journals and in 1974 he translated Mao Zedong's unpublished letters and speeches, which were published as *Mao Tse-tung Unrehearsed*.